Joseph Meadows Cowper, Robert Crowley

The Select Works of Robert Crowley

Joseph Meadows Cowper, Robert Crowley

The Select Works of Robert Crowley

ISBN/EAN: 9783337133993

Printed in Europe, USA, Canada, Australia, Japan

Cover: Foto ©ninafisch / pixelio.de

More available books at **www.hansebooks.com**

The Select Works

of

Robert Crowley

edited by

J. M. Cowper

EARLY ENGLISH TEXT SOCIETY

Extra Series, 15

1872

KRAUS REPRINT CO.

Millwood, New York

1975

The
Select Works of Robert Crowley.

Early English Text Society.

Extra Series. No. xv.

1872.

BERLIN: ASHER & CO., 13, UNTER DEN LINDEN.

NEW YORK: C. SCRIBNER & CO.; LEYPOLDT & HOLT.

PHILADELPHIA: J. B. LIPPINCOTT & CO.

The Select Works

of

Robert Crowley,

Printer, Archdeacon of Hereford (1559-1567),
Vicar of St Lawrence, Jewry, &c. &c.

NAMELY, HIS

EPIGRAMS, A.D. 1550; VOYCE OF THE LAST TRUMPET, A.D. 1550;
PLEASURE AND PAYNE, A.D. 1551; WAY TO WEALTH, A.D. 1550;
AN INFORMACION AND PETICION.

———————

EDITED

With Introduction, Notes, and Glossary,

BY

J. M. COWPER,

EDITOR OF 'ENGLAND IN THE REIGN OF KING HENRY THE EIGHTH,'
'THE TIMES' WHISTLE,' ETC.

LONDON:
PUBLISHED FOR THE EARLY ENGLISH TEXT SOCIETY
BY KEGAN PAUL, TRENCH, TRÜBNER & CO., LIMITED,
DRYDEN HOUSE, 43, GERRARD STREET, SOHO, W.
1872.

[Reprinted 1905.]

TO

My Sister Liz,

OF CLYRO, RADNORSHIRE,

I DEDICATE THIS VOLUME OF THE WORKS

OF THE OLD

ARCHDEACON OF HEREFORD.

CONTENTS.

ADDITIONS AND CORRECTIONS.

XV. CROWLEY'S SELECT WORKS.

On p. 73 is the stanza—

> And at the last thou shalt be founde
> To occupye a place only
> As do in Agime ziphres rounde,
> And to hynder learuyng greatlye.

The two words "Agime" and "ziphres" the editor does not explain. But *Agime* is a mere misprint for *Augrime*, and *ziphres* are *ciphers*. It is an old saying, and occurs in the poem of "Richard the redeles" (edited by Mr Wright with the title "Poem on the Deposition of Richard II.")[1]—

> "Than satte summe · as *siphre* doth in *awgrym*,
> That noteth a place · and no thing availith."
>
> Pass. iv. ll. 54, 55.

That is to say, there were some members of parliament who sat ever like ciphers in augrim (or arithmetic), which merely mark a place, though of no value in themselves.—W. W. SKEAT.

---

[1] The "Deposition of Richard II." is a false title, because the poem was obviously written (as Mr Wright himself says, by the way) before Richard was deposed. I give it the title "Richard the redeles," taken from the 1st line of the poem, "Now, Richard the *redeles*, reweth on ʒou-self." This reminds us of Ethelred, surnamed Unready, i. e. un-redy, redeles. And it preserves the *Richard* of the old title, under which it is naturally entered. There is allusion to the execution of Scrope, Bushy, and Green, July 29, 1399 ; and as Richard II. was deposed at the end of September, we get either August or September for the date of the composition of the poem : and if September, this would account for the sudden break-off of the poem. It was useless to go on giving the King good advice after that ; so William simply left off.—W. W. S.

INTRODUCTION.

ROBERT CROLE, Croleus, Crowlæus, or Crowley, is said to have been born in Gloucestershire, but the place of his birth and the condition of his parents are alike involved in obscurity. In or about the year 1534 he entered the University of Oxford and soon became a demy of Magdalene College. In 1542, having taken his degree of B.A., he was made a probationer-fellow. In 1549 he commenced printing in London, and carried on the business for about three years, the latest production of his press bearing date 1551.[1] His printing he carried on in Ely Rents, Holborn, where he earned the honour of being the first to print and publish "The Vision of William concerning Piers the Plowman," three different impressions of which were issued by Crowley in 1550.[2]

But printing did not absorb the whole of Crowley's energies. To his labours in disseminating knowledge by means of the press, he added the not less important—perhaps in his day, when books were dear and readers comparatively scarce, the more important—work of preaching in London and elsewhere, having been ordained a deacon by Ridley on 29th Sep. 1551.[3]

As soon as Mary succeeded to the throne of her brother, Crowley, with other English Protestants, retired to Frankfort, where they remained till her death rendered it safe for them to return to this country. Crowley's popularity as a preacher soon brought him into notice. In 1559 he was admitted to the Archdeaconry of Hereford,

---

[1] Collier, *Bib. Cat.* i. 489.   [2] *The Vision*, etc., ed. Skeat. xxxi.
[3] In Ridley's register Crowley is styled Stationer of the parish of St Andrew, Holborn. *Machyn's Diary*, Camd. Soc., n. p. 376.

and in the following year he was instituted to the Stall or Prebend of "Pratum Majus" in the Cathedral of that city.[1] On the 19th October, 1559, and again on the 31st March, 1561, he was the Preacher at Paul's Cross, and about this time he was parson of St Peter the Poor.[2]

In 1563 he was collated to the prebend of Mora in the Cathedral of St Paul, but was deprived in 1565.[3] In the following year he held the Vicarage of St Giles's, Cripplegate, of which he was deprived and prohibited from preaching or ministering the Sacraments within twenty miles of London. The causes which led to his deprivation are found in Abp Parker's Correspondence with Cecil,[4] from which it appears that Crowley and his curate expelled from the church divers clerks who were there in their surplices to bury a dead body. The clerks alleged that it was the custom, and that "my Lord of London" had commanded them to wear surplices within the churches. This gave rise to some tumult, and when Crowley appeared before Parker to answer for his behaviour, his conduct was such that the Archbishop "could do no less" than order him to be imprisoned in his own house. The Lord Mayor, too, lodged a complaint against Crowley, who answered "that he would not suffer the wolf"—"meaning the surplice man"—to come to his flock. This led to his further committal, and a Mr Bickley was sent to preach in his parish. In the further examination of Crowley it appears that he quarrelled with the singing men about their "porters' coats," that he said he would set them fast by the feet if they would break the peace, that he gave utterance to many "fond paradoxes that tended to Anabaptistical opinions, that he would preach until deprived, and that he would be deprived by order of the law." "But I dulled his glory," says Parker, who thought the suspension and secret prison would prove "some terror." In 1567 he is reported to have said that "he would not be persuaded to minister

---

[1] For the dates referring to Hereford, I am indebted to the kindness of the Rev. F. P. Havergal of the College, Hereford. To him my best thanks are due for his prompt attention to my letters on this subject.

[2] *Zurich Letters*, 2nd Series, 147, *n.* 6, Park. Soc. See also *Machyn's Diary.* pp. 215, 229.

[3] Lansd. MSS. 982, f. 104.

[4] *Parker's Correspondence*, Parker Society, pp. 275—278.

in those conjuring garments of popery," meaning the surplice, which seems to have been the cause of as much bickering three hundred years ago as it is now.[1]

During his suspension he was ordered to remain with the Bishop of Ely, but after a time he was permitted to return to London for twelve days that he might put his household affairs in order, "provided always that during the time of his abode in London, he do not privily nor publicly preach, read, nor minister the Sacraments," except licensed so to do by the Archbishop of Canterbury and the Bishop of London. In 1567 he resigned his Archdeaconry, and in the next year (1568) he was succeeded in his prebendal stall in Hereford Cathedral by another clerk. On the 5th May, 1576, Crowley was collated to the Vicarage of St Lawrence, Jewry,[2] but this he resigned in 1578.[3] In 1580 he was appointed with another to confer with the Romanists confined in the Marshalsea and White Lion in Southwark. One of the prisoners "pulled a pamphlet out of his bosom, read it, and delivered it" to Crowley to be answered. The pamphlet was entitled "Six Reasons set down to show that it is no orderly way in controversies of faith to appeal to be tried only by the Scriptures (as the absurd opinion of all the Sectaries is), but the Sentence and Definition of the Catholic Church," etc. To this "I drew up," says Crowley, "an answer now published the 6th of January," 1580-1, entitled "An Answer to Six Reasons," etc.[4]

A Puritan of the narrowest school, he was constantly engaged in controversies upon religious matters, and his zeal in this respect must have been a sore trial to the Bishops. "His pulpit and his press," says Warton,[5] "those two prolific sources of faction, happily co-operated in propagating his principles of predestination : and his shop and his sermons were alike frequented. Possessed of those talents which qualified him for captivating the attention and moving the passions of the multitude, under Queen Elizabeth he held many

---

[1] Remains of Abp Grindal. Parker Society, p. 211.
[2] Lansd. MSS. 982, f. 104.
[3] T. Corser. Collect. Ang. Poet., pt iv. p. 540.
[4] Lansd. MSS. 982, f. 104.
[5] Hist. Eng. Poet., iii. 187. But Warton was not quite right, for it seems Crowley left off printing about the time of his ordination.

dignities in a Church whose doctrines and polity his undiscerning zeal had a tendency to destroy." He seems to have preached anywhere, under any circumstances; at one time before Bonner's prison door, when the haughty prelate was confined in the Marshalsea,[1] at other times at Paul's Cross, as we have seen above; now to a "grett audyens" at a funeral, and soon after at Bow on occasion of the marriage of "Master Starke to the dowthur of Master Allen."[2] He closed his long and active but stormy career in 1588, when about 70 years of age, and was buried in the church of St Giles,[3] Cripplegate, of which, two and twenty years before, he had been vicar.

For further particulars of Crowley and references to him and his works, the reader may consult Lansd. MSS. 9 ff. 157—162; Ib. 982, ff. 94, 104; *Writings of Bradford*, Parker Society, ii. 207, n. 3; *Tyndale's Answer to More*, etc., Parker Society, p. 220; *Fulke's Answers*, Parker Society, p. 3; Strype's *Eccles. Mem.* ii. pt 2, pp. 465—472; Wood's *Athenæ Oxon.*; Warton's *Hist. Eng. Poetry*; Tanner's *Bibliotheca*, p. 210; Herbert's *Ames*, p. 757; Collier's *Bib. Cat.* i. 489; Skeat's Intro. to the V. of P. the Plowman; W. Carew Hazlitt's Hand-Book; and Corser's *Collectanea Anglo-Poetica*, pt iv.

To give a mere outline of the numerous Pamphlets, Sermons, Answers, &c., which came from Crowley's pen would occupy more space than I have at my command, and more time than I should care to give. Those who are desirous to know more than this brief Introduction contains will find their labours somewhat lightened by the references to books given above.

The Five Tracts printed in this volume are thought to be the most interesting as they are the most valuable, historically speaking, of the old Puritan's writings. Laying aside, as much as such a man could lay aside, his controversial nature in these, he deals with the faults, the weaknesses, the trials, the wrongs, the foolishnesses of his countrymen, and causes the different classes of men to stand and live before us.

---

[1] T. Corser, *Collect. Ang. Poet.*, pt iv. p. 540.
[2] See *Machyn's Diary*, Camd. Soc. pp. 269, 278, 295, 311.
[3] His Epitaph is given in Dibdin's Herbert's *Ames*, iv. 326, note—
"Here lieth the body of Robert Crowley Clerk, vicar of this Parish, who departed this Life the 18th daie of June Anno Dñi. 1588.

Taking these tracts in the order in which they stand in this volume we have—

(1.) *One and Thyrtie Epigrammes, wherein are bryefly touched so many Abuses that maye and ought to be put away.* 1550.

These Epigrams were thought to be lost. Even the indefatigable W. Carew Hazlitt did not know of a copy, and they were chiefly remembered from fifteen quoted by Strype.[1] But Mr Furnivall was fortunate enough to discover a copy in the Cambridge University Library.[2] This is the only copy which is known to be in existence.

Why " one and thirty " it is difficult to say, as there are " three and thirty " in addition to " The Boke to the Reader." First the Abbeys come under notice, and the writer could not fail to see what an opportunity had been lost for restoring them to their original purposes as fountains of learning and of relief to the poor and needy. We all know how Henry laid his iron grasp on the property of the Religious Houses, and how he was encouraged in his evil designs by the crowd of sycophants who hoped, and not in vain, that some of the crumbs which fell from him might drop into their laps. The simple people, encouraged with the prospect of seeing better days, acquiesced in the spoliation, and saw, when too late, how they had been deprived of their birthright without the poor consolation of the " mess of pottage " which is usually the reward of men who barter away that which their fathers have painfully gained.[3] The poor expected to profit by the suppression of the Abbeys, but how their hopes were dashed has been already pointed out.[4]

The alleys of two kinds, the bowling alleys and the alleys in which the hordes of miserable wretches, driven from their homes in

---

[1] *Ecc. Mem.* ii. pt 2, p. 465—472. The fifteen quoted by Strype are those commencing on pages 7, 8, 9, 12, 13, 14, 17, 20, 27, 33, 43, 45, 47, 48, and 49.

[2] The proofs have been read with the original by Mr D. Hall of Cambridge.

[3] For valuable information on the purposes of endowments the reader is referred to Mr Toulmin Smith's *The Parish*, 2nd ed. 1857, pp. 28, 30, 95, 597 —604. For directing my attention to this work, and for the loan of a copy, as well as for other valuable aid, I have to tender my best thanks to Miss Lucy Toulmin Smith.

[4] See *A Supplication of the Poore Commons* in "Four Supplications," ed. Furnivall and Cowper, pp. 79, 80 ; *Westminster Review*, No. lxxvii, January, 1871, p. 101 ; and the *Complaynt of Roderyck Mors*, to be edited for this Series.

the country to beg their daily bread in London, sheltered themselves at night, present a picture of London life not yet extinct. Then it must have been horrible. It is curious to notice how long it takes to remove what all men are willing to acknowledge abuses. The streets of London at that time were little better, perhaps no better, than narrow lanes, undrained, often unpaved, unlighted, and the nightly receptacles of filth of all kinds. Now our streets are better. We strike out a new street through the most densely populated districts, such as Tothill Fields, Westminster, and we build a row of magnificent houses on each side. We let in the light, but do we care to follow with our eyes the darkness which has been made more dark? Do we care to inquire what becomes of the thousands who, thronging the district before, are now compelled to huddle more closely than ever, inasmuch as, while their numbers are ever on the increase, the space allowed for them is diminished? Until we provide homes for the poor who are to be unhoused, before we make these gigantic improvements, we are far from acting up to our convictions and our knowledge.[1]

But moralizing is not our duty—we can see with our own eyes the bawds, the beggars, honest and dishonest; the swearers we can hear, the drunkards, the liars, the gamblers, the flatterers, the fools, the godless, the idle—many from necessity, not a few from choice ; the "inventors of strange news," the men who hold divers offices— the "double-beneficed men," who, in our day, are not so often found in the ranks of the clergy as they are in the ranks of the army, where nothing seems more common than "double benefices," one civil, the other military ; the "nice" women with their hair dyed and laid out in "tussocks as big as a ball;" the vain writers, the vain talkers, and vain hearers, how they all stand forth in our own day, more refined, changed in dress, changed in manners, but how like! Are we *much* better than those whom Crowley sketched upwards of three hundred years ago? Let the reader read and judge.[2]

(2.) *The Voyce of the Last Trumpet* . . . . *callyng al estats of*

---

[1] See note, p. xxiv.

[2] For the condition of Scotland about this time refer to Mr Furnivall's Preface to *The Minor Poems of William Lauder*, E. E. T. S., 1870.

men to the ryght path of theyr vocation, etc., printed in 1550, is a
kind of metrical sermon containing twelve lessons addressed "to
twelve several estates of men." Wood[1] says, "The said [John]
Plough also wrote . . . The Sound of the Doleful Trumpet"—but
when or where it was printed "I cannot tell, for I have not seen" it.
I do not find the name of Plough in Bohn's *Lowndes*. The title
given by Wood sounds very much like our "Voice of the Last
Trumpet."

The unique copy which we have used was kindly placed at the
disposal of the E. E. T. S. by Mr F. S. Ellis, of 33, King Street,
Covent Garden, in whose possession it was, but it has since been
purchased for the British Museum. The edges have been cut and
many of the references to texts of Holy Writ destroyed. These I
have supplied as nearly as I could, denoting letters and numerals so
supplied by placing them in brackets. Sometimes the reader may
doubt the accuracy of my references, and I shall not be surprised, for
I am by no means convinced that I have given those which were
lost. The vagueness of some of them, and the fact that they were
taken from an early version of the Bible, rendered the task by no
means an easy one.

In the "Book to the Reader" Crowley confesses that though he
barks at the faults of men, he is unwilling to bite if he can accom-
plish any good by barking. The aim of the Sermon is to inculcate
a spirit of obedience and submission in those who are under subjec-
tion, on the principle that "whatever is, is best." In the Epigram
on Beggars (p. 14) he would make the lazy work, and he exposes some
of their tricks, but here he seems only to deal with those who were
beggars by compulsion. There is something of the ludicrous in the
tone he assumes towards these poor creatures, but there is no reason
to think he was "chaffing" them :—

> "Thus leave I thee in thy calling,
> Exhorting thee therein to stand ;
> And doubtless at thy last ending
> Thou shalt be crowned at God's hand."—(p. 59.)

The same spirit pervades the Servant's Lesson (p. 59) and the

[1] *Athenæ Oxon.*, fol. 126.

Yeoman's (p. 63). They are to bear all, to do all, and to possess their souls in patience, looking for no change in this world, unless one for the worse! The servant who is "sturdy and does his service with grudging" is promised scourging, drudgery, slavery, and, if he runs away, a worse master than the one he has left. Crowley's advice is excellent, but in the then condition of things "flesh and blood," it is to be feared, often rebelled against it.

The yeoman is to "plow, plant, and sow;" to beware of even the wish to rise; to be charitable and contented. If he dared to hoard up riches, God's wrath was threatened. Hardest of all, if his landlord raised his rent (and how universal the practice!) he was enjoined to pay it, and to pray for his oppressor! The doctrine of absolute submission is taught in all its ugly deformity, with the addition of the divine right of kings.

The unlearned priest (p. 70) is severely handled for his ignorance, his immorality, and his false doctrine. The wide-spread hope that the Mass would be restored is referred to—

> " Put not the ignorant in hope,
>   That they shall see all up again
>   That hath been brought in by the Pope,
>   And all the preachers put to pain."

Yet three short years saw "all up again," and the preachers not only put to pain, but Crowley himself fleeing for his life, and "putting the sea between" him and his Queen. But there is one gem of advice, applicable not merely to the unlearned priests of Crowley's time, but to learned and unlearned of all times—

> " Be ever doing what thou can,
>   Teaching or learning some good thing,
>   And then, like a good Christian,
>   Thou dost walk forth in thy calling."

The Scholar's Lesson is interesting as giving a glimpse of that muscular education which, as a nation, we are only now beginning to learn afresh. The scholar was to "recreate his mind" by fishing, fowling, hunting, hawking; while trials of strength, skill, speed— still to recreate the mind—were to be made in shooting, bowling, casting the bar, tennis, tossing the ball, and running base like men of war[1] (p. 73). The whole lesson contains good advice and is quite worthy of its author.

Learned men, it appears, were not faultless. It is implied that they lived dissolutely and needed amendment of life as much as others. They seem to have had failings in the matters of dress, usury, and simony. This Learned Man's Lesson applies to clergy and laity alike.

The physician is severely dealt with. Covetous of gain and ignorant, he neglected the poor for the sake of the rich. A quarter of a century later, in *Newes out of Powles Churchyarde*, there was ground for similar charges. In the *Newes* the physicians are ranked next to the lawyers, and

" *Vnguentum Aureum*, or suchlyke,"[2]

was required to make them hasten to see their patients. They gained money, but no man knew how they spent it, and no man heard of any good deeds that they did. The Lawyer here follows the physician —generally where any ill was to be said, the lawyer took the lion's share, or, at all events, an equal share with the clergy. Crowley in this lesson taxes them with an insatiable greed, with bawling like beasts, and warns them to assist the poor as well as the rich, to fear no man's power, to do justice to all men, to show no favour. The old charges of bribery are brought against them in the *Newes out of Powles*[3] and in the *Times' Whistle*,[4] but in these two works we get a redeeming feature : *all are not corrupt* :—

" I know, friend Bertulph, some there be
Whose hands regard no meed,
Whose hearts dye no deceit at all,
From whom no harms proceed.

---

[1] Henry VIII., it is said, after his accession to the throne retained the casting of the bar among his favourite amusements. At the commencement of the seventeenth century such athletic games were by no means "beseeming of nobility."

Base, or Prisoners' Bars, a game, success in which depended upon the agility and skill in running. The game is still known in Kent under the name of Prisoners' Base. In the reign of Edward III. it was prohibited to be played in the avenues of Westminster Palace. A game exceedingly popular among the young men of this part of Kent, and known as "Goal Running," seems to be a modification of the ancient game of Base. For further information, see Strutt's *Sports and Pastimes.*

[2] *Newes out of Powles*, &c., Sat. 3 (1576).   [3] Sat. 2.   [4] p. 42.

And sure I am when cause of truth
Before such men is tried,
With simple truth they justice yield
And justly do decide."[1]

And the *Times' Whistle*:

" And you, which should true equity dispense,
Yet bear a gold-corrupted conscience,
Looke for some plague vpon your heads to light,
That suffer rich wrong to oppresse poore right.
All lawyers I cannot heerof accuse,
For some there are that doe a conscience vse
In their profession. This our land containes
Some in whose heart devine Astræa raignes.
To these, whose vertue keeps our land in peace,
I wish all good, all happines encrease.
Go forward then, and with impartiall hands
Hold iustice ballance in faire Albians lands."[2]

The Merchant, the Gentleman, and the Magistrate come next in order, the shortcomings of each being pointed out, and the results of their wrong-doing laid before us.

The Woman's Lesson comes last. It is the old, old story—they would talk, dress, dye their hair, paint their faces ; they ought to be modest, obedient, industrious, and to see that their children were well brought up, and their servants cared for.

(3.) *Pleasure and Payne*, etc., is dedicated to Lady Dame Elizabeth Fane, wife of Sir Ralph Fane, Knight,[3] and from this dedication we learn that Crowley's object in writing this was to cause men " to stay at the least way, and not proceed any further in the inventing of new ways to oppress the poor of this realm, whose oppression doth already cry unto the Lord for vengeance" (p. 108).

My attention was drawn to this " excessively rare metrical tract" by the mention of it in the *Collectanea Anglo-Poetica* of Mr Corser, who was in possession of a copy. Our reprint is taken from a copy

---

[1] *Newes out of Powles*, &c., Sat. 2.

[2] p. 50. For more on lawyers and bribery see my Preface to *England in the Reign of Henry VIII.*, pp. cxv.—cxviii.

[3] A Sir Ralph Fane, knight banneret, is mentioned in the Patent Rolls of Edward VI. Crowley was the first Englishman who versified the whole Psalter. In this work he may have been assisted by Lady Elizabeth Fane, for in Dibdin's *Typ. Ant.* iv. 331 *n.*, mention is made of the Lady Elizabeth Fane's 21 *Psalms* and 102 Proverbs. See note, p. xxviii.

in the Bodleian Library.[1] It has been found more convenient to print two lines in one than to follow the original, which runs—

> "When Christ shall come
>   to iuge vs all,
>   His Fathers frendis
>   then will he call."

This alteration of the lines and the revision of the punctuation and the use of capitals are the only liberties which have been taken with the Bodleian copy. And here it may be remarked that, as far as punctuation and the use of capitals are concerned, an endeavour has been made to conform to modern use in the whole of these tracts.[2]

There is no necessity to enter into any detailed account of subjects dealt with in this tract. The reader who cares to know, and once begins to read it, will not lay it down until he has finished the task.

(4.) *The Way to Wealth, wherein is plainly taught a most present Remedy for Sedicion*,[3] is the most important of Crowley's works, inasmuch as it enters more deeply into the causes which led to the disturbances in Edward's days, and the means by which the condition of the poor might be ameliorated—it "holds the candle" to the men who had the power and the will to root up "the stinking weed of Sedition," which was rapidly spreading its poisonous influences over the land.

It is needless here to go over the history of the country during the twenty years which preceded the appearance of the *Way to Wealth* (1530—1550). The suppression of the abbeys, the casting loose upon the country—often homeless and almost always friendless —the men and women who by their education and living were unfitted to cope with the outer world and earn their daily bread; the grievous disappointment of the many who hoped for some other and better relief than they had obtained from the monks; the cruel spirit of oppression which took possession of the men who reaped

---

[1] Mr G. Parker read the proofs with the original.

[2] This modernizing of the punctuation and the making the use of capital letters uniform are the only things to be desired in Mr Arber's most valuable Reprints.

[3] From the Bodleian copy. The proofs were read with the original by Mr G. Parker.

the advantage of the change from the old order of things ;—all these
may be seen by a reference to books which are in the hands of the
readers of these "Texts," and Mr Furnivall's *Ballads from Manu-
scripts.*[1] Still those who have read so far will do well to read with
increased care this passionate appeal of the old Puritan, who stands
up and boldly rebukes the wrong-doer; whether he be the king on
his throne, or the beggar dying by the wayside of hunger, and disease,
and neglect. The farmers, the graziers, the butchers, the lawyers,
the merchants, the gentlemen, the knights, the lords—all who lived
as "cormorants and gulls," by the plunder and oppression of the
poor and needy—are here called to account, and have their misdeeds
placed before them, and the charges which were commonly made
against them by the suffering poor proclaimed in powerful language.
That Crowley pitied these men, and longed to improve their condition is beyond doubt. But he could see and had the courage to

---

[1] "It has been already shown that an essential and principal part of
the first bestowal and purpose of those endowments which have now become
entirely diverted to ecclesiastical purposes, or engrossed by lay impropriators,
was the relief of the poor. The task of that relief was thus made a local one ;
and it was committed in each place to those who had the two counter checks
continually present, of self-interest not to promote or yield to extravagance,
and of the continual liability to be presented, by those not then 'excused,'
for unfaithfulness, if they neglected what true need required.

"Under cover of the 'Reformation,' Henry VIII. got to himself a vast
proportion of what was thus expressly given in trust for the poor. He got it
under false pretences [quotes Coke, 4th Inst. p. 44]. He gave it to his favourites,
in breach of honour, honesty, and his pledged faith. This monstrous pillage
of the poor, and gross fraud upon the nation, produced an immediate effect.
The real and deserving poor, robbed of what was thus from of old set apart to
meet their true needs, were flung upon society. Vagrancy had thus everywhere a colourable excuse given to it, and soon largely increased. Instead of
the true remedy being applied, and a part of what had been wrongfully mis-
appropriated being restored, a new burthen was cast upon the country for the
support of the poor as a class. Thenceforth 'pauperism' became a caste in
England.

"It is not surprising that, under the anomalous state of things thus arising,
anomalies were created in the endeavour to meet it. Acts distinguished by
their attempts to keep down the natural fruits of such wrong-doing by force,
terror, and barbarity, were passed, altered, and repealed. It was attempted
—however paradoxical it may sound—to enforce voluntary alms. Almost the
only provision that can be said to be marked by wisdom, is one found in an
Act of 27 Henry VIII. cap. 25, which forbad the giving of alms in money, except to the common fund, or 'Stock,' of the parish or other place. In the
same Act is found the first suggestion as to Overseers," &c., &c.—*The Parish,*
by Toulmin Smith, 2nd edition, p. 144, 145.

declare that, though oppressed and trodden underfoot, they were not free from blame, and he endeavours to soothe their rebellious spirits by reasoning with them and arguing with them, and showing them that their open resistance to authority only put a whip into the hands of the rich who sought excuses for their evil deeds.

Not only were the poor commons pilled and polled by the rich laity, but, worst of all, the reformed clergy, the bishops, deans, archdeacons, canons, parsons, and vicars were intent upon grasping all the wealth within their reach. They ate the fat and decked themselves with the wool, but the simple sheep were left untended and unfed in the wilderness. The sorrowful and sad were left uncomforted, the sick unhealed, the broken not bound up, the wanderers unrestored. Churchmen were busy, but it was in obtaining lands for their heirs and fine-fingered ladies, who were clothed in "fine frocks and French hoods," but were naked "of al pointes of honest housewifery." Things were bad enough before the Reformation, and it is no consolation to say so, but surely they must have appeared worse after it, when men had the Bible in their own hands, and were unable to lay all the odium at the door of "the Pope and his shavelings." Religion and the Bible were not to blame for this state of things. Men by a violent effort had shaken off the yoke, and, being free, were ignorant how to use their freedom to the common advantage, and so they used it in oppression and wrong. It had been so before, and it has been so since. The oppressed set free is apt to become the oppressor.

Crowley taxes the curates with having "been the stirrers-up of the simple people in the late tumults," a not unlikely charge to be brought against a body of men who by their virtues and learning had not yet won the esteem of their countrymen. Nor was it unlikely that they did so. The Church, wisely or unwisely, has often had the courage to enter its protest against the oppressions of the mighty, but in this case caution is necessary in accepting the charge as true. Such abject submission as Crowley taught, has, luckily for us, not been common among our religious teachers; if it had our bondage might have been worse than Egyptian.

The whole is a masterly discourse, and will be read with much interest as a sketch made by an eye-witness of the condition of things described in it.

(5.) *An Informacion and Peticion agaynst the oppressours of the pore Commons of this Realme* is a Petition to the Parliament of Edward VI. Of the many subjects which will have to be discussed, Crowley can see none demanding speedier attention than the oppres sions under which the "pore commones" groaned, clergy and laity uniting to inflict the most cruel wrongs. Religious matters too demanded redress, because, while the people were ignorant and superstitious, the clergy were more apt to play the butcher than the shepherd. They abused the rites and sacraments of the Church, using them as matters of merchandise, the clergy of London setting the example.

The possessioners, leasemongers, and landlords, "making the uttermost penny of all their grounds," exacting unreasonable fines, and racking their rents, receive scant mercy at Crowley's hands. It was a time for plain speaking even in the churches, as the following extract from "The Prayer for Landlords," in one of Edward's Liturgies, will show :—

"We heartily pray Thee that they (who possess the grounds, pastures, and dwelling-places of the earth) may not rack and stretch out the rents of their houses and lands, nor yet take unreasonable fines and incomes after the manner of covetous worldlings, but so let them out to others that the inhabitants thereof may both be able to pay the rents and also honestly to live, to nourish their families, and to relieve the poor. . . . Give them grace also that they may be content with that that is sufficient, and not join house to house nor couple land to land to the impoverishment of other, but so behave themselves in letting out their tenements, lands, and pastures, that after this life they may be received into everlasting dwelling-places."

The mischiefs which flowed out of "this more than Turkish tyranny" are graphically described. The honest householders reduced to the condition of menials ; the honest matrons to the "needy rock and cards ;" the men children of good hope, driven to handycrafts and day labour ; the chaste virgins, to marry perpetual poverty, the immodest to Bankside, the stubborn, after a life of crime and misery, to the gallows ; the universal destruction which "chances to this noble realm !"

In conclusion, I wish to express my thankfulness that it has fallen to my lot to prepare these Reformation Tracts for the press, however unworthily I may have performed my task. Often disagreeing with the writers, often doubting the truthfulness of the charges brought by foes against foes, I have learnt to receive alike with caution the glowing accounts given by some of the condition of the people, and the crimes and neglect laid at the door of the vanquished by the successful. Robbery and recrimination were all too common. The State plundered the Church, taxing it with every conceivable crime; the rich plundered the poor, charging them with harbouring seditious designs; the Puritan taxed the papist with idleness, ignorance, and immorality, and when he had gained his churches and his tithes, proceeded to open the doors to "seven other spirits," each of which was worse than the one driven out; and the poor man, plundered by all, and suffering from the divisions and quarrels of the classes above him, endured in his own body all the calamities which could befall a man. The times are times we should study, not envy; and if now and again we feel a tingle of shame in our cheeks at what our Protestant forefathers were guilty of in their gigantic work, we may ask ourselves whether, if the task fell to our lot, with all our intelligence and all our enlightenment and all our science, we should have been likely to do it better. They did what they could—imperfectly, with motives and by means which will not always bear examination. Let us be thankful, and do the part which remains to us.

J. M. COWPER.

Davington Hill, Faversham, 1871.

NOTES.

Sunday drinking, &c., page 9. "What should I tell men in manye words, that which al men see & feele in continual & lamentable experience. Go to alehouses on the Saboth daies, there is as well sold all kinde of loosenesse as vitayles. Go to Greenes, there is myrth that would wounde a Christian mans heart with heauinesse. Goe to Fayres, there is a shewe and traffike, as well of all lewdnesse, as of wares. Yea, goe to all other places, both in City and countrey, and what shall you see, but so many euils that prouoke God, to the powryng forth of most fearefull iudgements, the Theaters, Parish garden, Tauernes, streetes, fieldes, all full and prophanely occupied, and this chiefly on the Saboth day."—*The Vnlawfull Practises Of Prelates Against Godly Ministers,* &c., sig. B. 3, back, ab. 1584. There is a copy of this small work in the Canterbury Cathedral Library, Shelf Mk. Z. 9. 28.

Homes of the Poor, pp. xiv., 10. The following "cuttings" from the *Standard* of April 6 and 7, 1871, are worth preserving. It is only fair to add that "official explanations proved" that the man had no grievance whatever!

"GUILDHALL.

"ATTEMPTED SUICIDE THROUGH THE STRINGENT CITY POLICE REGULATIONS.—*Mary Ann Folkard,* the wife of one of the City police-constables, was charged before Sir Thomas Gabriel with attempting to commit suicide by endeavouring to throw herself from Paul's Wharf into the river.

"Mr Alfred Oxley said he lived at 49, Gloucester-street, St John's-road, Hoxton, and about half-past one o'clock the previous day he saw the prisoner on Paul's Wharf trying to get away from her daughter so that she might throw herself into the river. He assisted in stopping her, and gave her into custody. At the station she said that she was not drunk, she knew what she was about, and that it was her intention to commit the act.

"Sir Thomas Gabriel asked her why she did it.

"The Prisoner (a very respectable-looking woman) said she would not have done it if she had had a home to go to.

" Folkard, the husband of the prisoner, was called forward, and, in reply to Sir Thomas Gabriel, said that his wife was a most sober, steady, industrious woman, and had never made any attempt on her life before. The reason she had done so now was, because they could not find a home to go to. By the City police regulations they were bound to live within the City boundary, and in consequence of the many poor houses that had been pulled down for railways and improvements they were not able to find a place to live in. He first took a place that was not fit for a dog to live in, until he got a house, and he stayed in that until the roof was taken off and the dust from the ceiling fell on their heads and compelled them to leave. The only place he could find was a large warehouse, where he and his family were permitted to live, and it was that, he believed, that had turned his wife's brain. To his knowledge four other constables were in the same condition as himself.

" Sir Thomas Gabriel said it was a very foolish thing of her to do, because if she had no lodging to-day she might have one to-morrow.

" Folkard said that was their difficulty ; they could not get lodgings in the City.

" Sir Thomas Gabriel said—Then why not live out of it ?

" Folkard replied that the police regulations would not let them live out of it.

" Sir Thomas Gabriel asked if he had made any representation of that to the Commissioner of Police.

" Mr Martin, the chief clerk, said they had not, for the policemen were afraid to make any representation.

" Sir Thomas Gabriel said he thought there ought to be some representation made to the police authorities, and he should see to it. Could they not live in those model lodging-houses ?

" Mr Martin thought they were all outside the City, and appealed to Inspector Foulger on that point.

" Inspector Foulger said they were.

" Sir Thomas Gabriel said—But surely some accommodation should be got for these men. He asked Inspector Foulger what objection there could be to the men living, for instance, in the model lodging-houses in the Farringdon-road ?

" Inspector Foulger said they were outside the City, and the regulations of the force did not permit them to live outside the City.

" Sir Thomas Gabriel asked whether they had not accommodation for the men within the City.

" Inspector Foulger replied that the number of houses that had been pulled down had rendered it very difficult for the officers to find accommodation for themselves, their wives, and families.

" Sir Thomas Gabriel said it was a pity they were not allowed to live out of the City.

" Inspector Foulger said that all round the City boundary there was ample accommodation for the men if they were permitted to avail themselves of it, and in many instances they would be able to live nearer to their duty than they were at present. For instance, a man living near Temple Bar might have to be on duty on Tower-hill, and, if permitted, might live just outside the boundary, within a few minutes' walk of his duty.

"Sir Thomas Gabriel asked Folkard if he would take his wife home and take care of her.

"Folkard said he would take her home, but as he had his duty to perform he could not take more care of her than he had done. She was a very good wife and mother.

"Sir Thomas Gabriel asked her if she would promise not to attempt to destroy herself again.

"The Prisoner said she would not if she had a home to go to.

"Sir Thomas Gabriel said he could not let her go while she was in that state of mind, and appealed to Inspector Foulger as to whether a home could not be got for her.

"Inspector Foulger said that plenty could be got for her outside the City, but they were not permitted to take them on account of the police regulations.

"Sir Thomas Gabriel said he should remand the prisoner, and in the mean time communicate with Colonel Fraser, to see what could be done, in order to allow the police proper accommodation.

"The Prisoner was then remanded."

"As strange a story perhaps as was ever related in that great rival to works of melodramatic fiction, a police court, was narrated on Wednesday at Guildhall. The wife of a City police constable was charged before Alderman Sir Thomas Gabriel with attempting to commit suicide by flinging herself into the river from Paul's Wharf; and it was with difficulty that she had been rescued. When asked her motive for the desperate act, she replied that she would not have tried to kill herself if she had possessed a home to go to. Her husband told the Alderman that she was a sober, steady, and industrious woman, and had never before attempted suicide; but she had been reduced to despair through the want of a home. By the City police regulations the constables are bound to reside within the civic boundaries, and, according to the prisoner's husband, so many houses of the poorer class have been pulled down for railway and street improvements that the married policemen were quite unable to find such tenements as they could afford to rent. This man had first found a place 'not fit for a dog;' next he got into a house and stayed there until the roof was taken off and the hovel filled with dust and cinders from the railway; and then he and his family took shelter in a deserted warehouse. There were four other constables, he said, in a similarly homeless condition. 'Why not live out of the City?' asked logical Sir Thomas Gabriel. 'Because the police regulations will not allow us to do so,' replied the equally logical constable; and his statement seems to have been confirmed by Mr Martin, the chief clerk, who added that the constables were afraid to

make any representations of their grievances to the Commissioner of the
City Police. There were model lodging-houses in plenty available as
residences for policemen and their families ; but they were beyond the
City boundaries. Inspector Foulger, a very well-known and deserving
officer of the City Police, spoke even more strongly as to the sad plight
of the homeless constables. The Alderman asked the woman if she
would promise not to attempt to kill herself again, but she only replied
conditionally, ' that she would not do so again if she had a home to go
to.' At last, as it seemed, fairly puzzled, Sir Thomas remanded the
prisoner, saying that in the mean time he would communicate with
Colonel Fraser to see what could be done in order to allow the police
proper accommodation. Until we hear what Colonel Fraser has said to
Sir Thomas Gabriel, and how this wonderful Gordian knot of Blue Tape
is to be cut or unravelled, it would be difficult to fix upon the right
moral of this truly strange tale."

Paris Garden, p. 17. The place where the bears were kept and
baited. It was so named because Robert de Paris had a house and
garden there in the time of Rich. II., who ordered the butchers to purchase the garden that their refuse might be placed there. Paris Garden
seems to have been first used for bear baiting in the time of Henry
VIII. In 1583 a fearful accident happened there on a Sunday, when
the stage fell, killing and wounding great numbers. A detailed account
of this accident is given in the *Anatomie of Abuses* (p. 211) and several
contemporary writers. See Halliwell's *Arch. Dict.*, Collier's *Annals of
the Stage*, and the *Diary of Dr Dee*.

Swearing, pp. 18, 19. "They (the English) are also inconstant,
arrogant, vain-glorious, haughty-minded, and above all things inclined
to swearing, insomuch as if they speak but three or four words, yet
must they needs be interlaced with a bloody oath or two."—*Anatomie
of Abuses*, 1836, p. 147. For a later view of this detestable habit see
Times' Whistle, p. 24.

Wool, Tin, and Lead wrought within the realm, p. 38. For much information on imports and exports and suggestions for improving trade,
and through it the condition of the people, see *England in the Reign of
Henry VIII*.

Painting Faces, p. 44. "The women of Ailgna (many of them) use
to colour their faces with certain oils, liquors, unguents, and waters
made to that end, whereby they think their beauty is greatly decored."
—*Anatomie of Abuses*, 1836, p. 55. See also *The Times' Whistle*, pp.
24, 34.

Dress, pp. 44, 45. In the "Epistle Dedicatorie" to the *Anatomie
of Abuses*, the evils of the author's days are thus briefly touched upon :
" For as your Lordship knoweth, reformation of manners and amendment of life was never more needful ; for was pride (the chiefest argu-
ment of this book) ever so ripe ? Do not both men and women (for the
most part) every one in general, go attired in silks, velvets, damasks,
satins, and what not ? Which are attire only for the nobility and

gentry, and not for the other at any hand.   Are not unlawful games,
plays, interludes, and the like, everywhere frequented?   Is not whore-
dom, covetousness, usury, and the like, daily practised without all
punishment of law or execution of justice?" p. xi.

In the *Anatomie*, p. 17, it is said, "Now there is such a confuse
mingle mangle of apparel in Ailgna (Anglia), and such preposterous
excess thereof, as every one is permitted to flaunt it out in what apparel
he lusteth himself, or can get by any kind of means. So that it is very
hard to know who is noble, who is worshipful, who is a gentleman, who
is not." See also *Four Supplications*, and *England in the Reign of Henry
VIII.*, pp. clxxiv., 89, 90.

Rent-raisers, pp. xx., 46,

> "The landlord is a thief that racks his rents
> And mounts the price of rotten tenements,
> Almost unto a damned double rate,
> And such a thief as that[1] myself had late."
> > *Taylor's Works*, folio, 280, and *note*.

Lawyers, p. 82 ; *Judges*, p. 84. Consult *The Utopia, Ballads from
MSS, England in the Reign of Henry VIII.*, Latimer's *Sermons, Newes
out of Powles Churchyarde*, &c., on these topics.

Lady Elizabeth Fane, pp. xvi., 107.   Lady Elizabeth Fane's Psalms
and Proverbs were printed and published by Robert Crowley.   Sometimes the name appears as Vane. She has been supposed to be the wife
of the Sir Ralph Vane who was hung in 1551-2 as one of the principal
adherents of the Duke of Somerset.   She died 'at Holburne' and was
buried at St Andrew's, Holborn, on the 11th June 1568. For letters addressed to her by John Bradford, see Foxe, edit. 1631, iii. pp. 331, 332,
339.   See also Narratives of the Reformation, Camb. Soc., 1859, pp. 93,
94, 346.   For further references consult the General Index to the
Parker Society's Publications.

Poor in London, p. 116.   "There is a certain city in Ailgna[2] called
Munidnol[3] where as the poor lie in the streets upon pallets of straw, and
well if they have that too, or else in the mire and dirt as commonly it
is seen, having neither house to put in their heads, covering to keep
them from cold, nor yet to hide their shame withal, penny to buy them
sustenance, nor any thing else, but are suffered to die in the streets like
dogs or beasts, without any mercy or compassion showed to them at
all."—*Anatomie of Abuses*, 1836, p. 50.   Three hundred years have not
remedied matters.   The following are from the *Standard* of June 10 and
June 28, 1871 :—

"BOW-STREET.

" LIFE IN LONDON.—*James Lintott*, a ragged, shoeless young urchin
of about 13, with long matted hair, and with hands and features almost

---

[1] "One that eight years since bought many houses where I and many poor
men dwelt, and presently raised our rents from three pounds to five pounds."—
Taylor, ib.   [2] Anglia.   [3] Londinium.

untraceable through the dirt by which they were begrimed, was brought before Mr Vaughan, charged with being found in Somerset-street, Strand, with a box of flowers in his possession supposed to be stolen.

"Police-constable Sergeant, E division, stopped the boy at twelve o'clock at night. He said a chap gave him the box to take to a coffee-house in Hart-street, but he was walking in the opposite direction.

"It was proved that the box contained cut flowers worth 2l. 2s., and had been stolen from a van belonging to Mr Reeve, florist, Acton.

"Mr Vaughan, to prisoner.—Where do you live?

"Prisoner.—I don't live nowheres.

"Have you no friends in London?—No; I ain't got no friends.

"But where do you sleep at nights?—Under the show-board agin the Lyceum Theatre.

"Mr Vaughan.—What does he say?

"Gaoler.—He says he sleeps under the large posting board in front of the Lyceum Theatre.

"Mr Vaughan.—Do you mean by that you sleep there every night?

"Prisoner.—No, I don't sleep there every night. Sometimes I gits under other boards.

"But have you no home—no father or mother?—I has a father and mother, but they won't let me go home. When I goes home they turns me out agin. Father says he won't have me there.

"Why does he refuse to have you there?—'Cause I stopped out two or three nights, and then he wouldn't never take me back agin.

"Where does he live?—Over a boot-shop in Red Lion-street. I don't know the number.

"What is your father? Where does he work?—In Common Garden Market

"Gaoler.—He is a porter in the market, your worship.

"The prisoner was then remanded for a week."

"MANSION HOUSE.

"*John Stevens*, a boy in rags, eleven years of age, was charged under the Industrial Schools Act with having been found wandering, not having any home or settled place of abode or proper guardianship, or visible means of subsistence.

"The case was originally heard by Sir Robert Carden, about a week ago, and then, as now, excited considerable interest from being the first charge of the kind that had been preferred in the City of London since the Elementary Education Act came into operation. The complainant and only witness on the first occasion was Joseph Willes, who described himself as an industrial school officer to the London School Board. A week ago he found the boy wandering in Lower Thames-street about midday in a miserable plight, and asked him a few questions. The boy in reply said his mother had sent him out to beg, and that he was not to return home for a week; that his parents lived in the neighbourhood of the New Cut, Lambeth; that his father was 'sometimes an engineer and sometimes a cab driver;' that he had never been to any school, and that while he had been from home he had slept at nights, with about 20 other boys, under some tarpauling, and among empty fish-boxes in Billingsgate-market. The witness, thinking it a case contemplated by the Industrial Schools Act, and desiring to reclaim the boy from the streets, to have him educated and taught a trade by which he might gain his own living, took him to the Seething-lane Police-station, and had him formally charged. Sir Robert Carden, before whom the boy was first brought, commended the witness very much for the course he had taken, and expressed a hope that many scores of poor destitute children would be taken from the streets of the City, and educated and taught some handicraft by which they might earn an honest livelihood, adding that he himself had for years in his own way been a 'boy's beadle,' long before that expression was in use. The case was eventually adjourned to admit of the attendance of the boy's parents, Mr Oke, the chief clerk of the Lord Mayor, doubting whether it was one which exactly came within the meaning of the Industrial Schools Act, according to which a child to be dealt with according to its provisions must be without home or settled place of abode, or proper guardianship, or visible means of subsistence. Meanwhile the boy was sent to the union.

" Yesterday his mother, a poor but honest-looking woman, attended, and in answer to the Bench, said her husband was sometimes out of work; that she was a tailoress and worked hard to maintain the family, of whom there were three besides the boy in question, younger than he, and that she was willing to take him home and look after him, although, she added, if he preferred to be sent to school, she would be thankful. The boy himself, crying, begged that he might be allowed to go home.

" Mr Alderman Lusk said he was loth to separate parent and child, if the mother would promise to take care of the boy and do her duty to him.

" She gave the required undertaking, and was allowed to take her son away, after he had received an admonition from the Bench."

The reader may also consult Mr Furnivall's *Ballads from MSS.*, our *Four Supplications*, and my *England in the Reign of Henry VIII.*, &c., § 4, p. cx.

Patrons, p. 118 ; *Simony*, pp. 118, 120. In 1585 it was said, " For euen our plough boyes know it to be a common practise almost euery where amongst patrons, that either they take a great summe of mony, or mony worth, as it were a fine, with such sleighty conueiance, as if they were iuglers, that no man shal espy them or any law preuent them, or make some reseruation of the tithes and glebeland, as it were a rent, & many times all these practises be vsed togither, whose rauenous teeth, and also the paiment of the first fruites and tenthes, which the charge of their lawfull family, which the papists neuer knew, and also their tithes not paid them in so large a sise as heretofore hath bene done, hath brought the churchmen vnto such an ebbe, that after their death their executours doe not blesse them, except it be certaine of them which haue sundry benefices."—*A Lamentable Complaint of the Commonalty, By Way Of Svpplication, To The High Covrt Of Parliament, For A Learned Ministery.* In Anno. 1585, Sig. C. A copy is in the Canterbury Cathedral Library, Shelf Mk. Z. 9. 28.

Sedition, pp. 131, 141. "The breakefaste they had this laste somer" refers no doubt to the slaughter inflicted upon the rebels in the West and East of England in the summer of 1549, when half England was in a state of rebellion. See *Froude's History,* v.

This present Parliament, p. 153. The Parliament here referred to was most likely that which met in January, 1549. Its first measure was "An Act for the Uniformity of Service," &c. This "Informacion and Peticion" was probably published while this Parliament was sitting, and before the outbreak mentioned in *The Way to Wealth.*

The King's Visitation, p. 154. This visitation was made during Somerset's absence in Scotland. He returned to London from this expedition on the 8th October, 1547. See *Froude,* v. 56.

Articles, p. 170. These "Articles" were the "Six Articles." See my note to *Four Supplications,* p. 103.

Usury, p. 172. The Act legalising usury was passed, 37 H. VIII., c. 9, 1545. See *Four Supplications,* pp. 82, 84.

꧁ One and

thyrtye Epigrammes, wherein are

bryefly touched so many Abuses, that

maye and ought to be put away.

Compiled and Emprinted by

Robert Crowley, dwel-

lynge in Elye rentes

in Holburne.

Anno domini,

1550.

i. Cor. xiiii.
What so euer ye do, let the same be done to edifie wythall.

Gala. i.[1]
If I shoulde study to please men: than coulde I not
be the seruaunt of Christe.

Orig. vi.

CROWLEY.   1

3 ★

[Leaf ? back. is a blank.]

The Boke to the Reader. [leaf 3]

IF bokes may be bolde
   to blame and reproue
The faultes of all menne,
   boeth hyghe and lowe,   4
As the Prophetes dyd
   whom Gods Spirite did moue,
Than blame not myne Autor;
   for right well I knowe   8
Hys penne is not tempered
   vayne doctrine to sowe,
But as Esaye hath bydden,
   so muste he nedes crye,   12
And tell the Lordes people
   of their iniquitie.
     Nowe, if I do the worldelinges
   in anye poynte offende,   16
In that I reproue them
   for their wyckednes,
It is a plaine token
   they wyll not emende.   20
I take all the wyse men
   of the earth to wytnes
To them; therfore mine Autor
   biddeth me confesse,   24

Marginal notes:

If books may reprove faults

as the Prophets did, do not blame the Author.

Esai. 58.

He must tell the people of their sins.

If I offend men

it is clear they will not amend;

[leaf 3, back]

and since they
will not, he
accounts them
brands of hell.

That, sith they be determined
  styll in their synne to dwell,
He accounteth them no better
    than fire brandes of hell.   28
    Wherefore he bade me bid them
    holde them contente ;

He has not
written for such
as will not
amend,

He hath not written to them
  that will not emende ;   32
For to the willinge wicked
  no prophete shall be sente,
Excepte it be to tell them
  that, at the laste ende,   36

except to tell
them they will go
to the devil,

They shal be sure and certayne
  wyth Satanas to wende.
For before suche swyne
  no pearles maye be caste,   40
That in the filthye puddell
  take all their repaste.

but for such as
have no delight
in wickedness,

  To suche onely, therfore,
  I muste his message do,   44
As haue not their delite
  in wickednes to dwell ;

[leaf 4]

But when they heare their fault,
  are sorye they dyd so,   48

and such as
reform when they
hear their faults.

And louingely imbrace
  suche men as do them tell ;
Reformynge euermore
  their lyfe by the gospell,—   52
To these men am I sente,
  And these, I truste, will take

Such will take
the warning in
good part.

My warnynge in good parte,
  And their euill forsake.   56
    Iohn .viii.
He that is of God, heareth the
    worde of God.
    Finis.

Of Abbayes.

[leaf 4, back,
is a blank]

[leaf 5]

A S I walked alone,
   and mused on thynges
    That haue in my time

benc done by great kings,   60
I bethought me of Abbayes,
   that sometyme I sawe,
Whiche are nowe suppressed
   all by a lawe.   64

O Lorde (thought I then)
   what occasion was here,
To prouide for learninge
   And make pouertye chere ?   68

The landes and the jewels
   that hereby were hadde,
Would haue found godly prechers,
   which might well haue ladde   72
The people aright
   that now go astraye,
And haue fedde the pore,
   that famishe euerye daye.   76
But, as I thus thought,
   it came to my mynde,
That the people wyll not see,
   but delyte to be blynde.   80

Wherefore they are not worthy
   good prechars to haue,
Nor yet to be prouided for,
   but styll in vayne to craue.   84
Than sayde I (O Lorde God)
   make this tyme shorte,
For theyr sake onlye, Lorde,
   that be thy chosen sorte.   88

Math. 24

Of Alehouses.

NEdes must we haue places
    for vitayls to be solde,
for such as be sycke,
    pore, feble, and olde.   92
But, Lorde, to howe greate
    abuse they be growne !

In eche lyttle hamlet,
    vyllage, and towne,   96
They are become places
    of waste and excesse,
And herbour for such men
    as lyue in idlenes.   100

And lyghtly in the contrey
    they be placed so,
That they stande in mens waye
    when they shoulde to church go.   104

And then such as loue not
    to hear theyr fautes tolde,
By the minister that readeth
    the newe Testament and olde,   108
do turne into the alehouse,
    and let the church go ;
Yea, and men accompted wyse
    and honeste do so.   112

But London (God be praysed)
    all men maye commende,
Whych doeth nowe this greate
    enormitie emende.   116

For in seruice tyme
    no dore standeth vp,
Where such men are wonte
    to fyll can and cuppe.   120

[1] The side-notes of the original are printed in Italic throughout.

Wolde God in the countrey
 they woulde do the same,
Either for Gods feare,
 or for worldly shame !   124

Would that the
country would
do so.

How hallow they the Saboth,
 that do the tyme spende
In drynkinge and idlenes
 tyll the daye be at an ende? 128

[leaf 6, back]
They who spend
the Sabbath in
drinking do
worse than those
who plow.

Not so well as he doeth,
 that goeth to the plowe,
Or pitcheth vp the sheues
 from the carte to the mowe. 132

But he doeth make holye
 the Sabothe in dede,
That heareth Goddes worde,
 and helpeth suche as nede. 136

Luke[1] *xiii.*
He keeps it best
who does works
of need.

Of Allayes.

TWo sortes of Allayes
 in London I finde ;—
The one agaynste the lawe,
 and the other againste kinde. 140

Two sorts of
alleys in Lon-
don—

The firste is where bowlinge
 forbidden, men vse,
And, wastynge theyr goodes,
 do their laboure refuse. 144

bowling-alleys, in
which men waste
their goods.

But in London (alas !)
 some men are deuillishelye
Suffered to professe it,
 as an arte to lyue by. 148

*A dispraise
of London.*
Some live by the
game, and pro-
[leaf 7]
fess it as an art.

Well, I wyll saye no more,
 but suche as lyue so,
And officers that suffer them,
 shall togither go 152

These and those
who allow it

   [1] Orig. Mat.

will go to their
father Satan.
To Satan their sire,
    for of God they are not,
Who commaundeth to laboure

Exo. xxiii.
    syxe dayes, ye wotte,   156
And the seuenth he commaundeth
    all menne to sanctifie,
In beynge well occupied,
    and not idlelye.   160

*Allayes
agaynste
kynde.*
The other sort
of alleys make a
man weep.
The other sorte of Allayes,
    that be agaynste kynde,
Do make my harte wepe
    whan they come to my mind.   164

In them are poor
beggars innumer-
able.
For there are pore people,
    welmoste innumerable,
That are dryuen to begge,
    and yet to worcke they are able,   168
If they might haue al thinges
    prouided aright.

[leaf 7, back]
Alas! is not thys
    a greate ouer syght?   172

You Aldermen
that take the
rents,
Ye Aldermen and other,
    that take Allaye rente,
Why bestowe ye not the riches,
    that God hath you sente   176
In woule or in flaxe,

why don't you
find work for
these poor ones?
    to finde them occupied,
That nowe lye and begge
    by euerye highe waye side?   180
And you that be chiefe,
    and haue the commune treasure,
Why can you neuer finde
    a time of leasure,   184
To se where the treasure
    will finde them workinge,
To the profit of the Citye,
    in some maner thinge?   188

But (alas !) this my tale
   is to deafe men tolde ;
For the charitie of rich men
   is nowe thorowe colde.   192

Alas ! I talk to deaf men, for rich men's charity is cold.

And this is a Citye
   in name, but, in dede,
It is a packe of people
   that seke after meede ;   196
For Officers and al
   do seke their owne gaine,
But for the wealth of *the* commons
   not one taketh paine.   200

Loke the definition of a Citie, you [leaf 8] *that be lerned.* The City is a pack of people all seeking gain.

An hell with out order,
   I maye it well call,
Where euerye man is for him selfe,
   And no manne for all.   204

It is a hell without order, where every man is for himself.

Of Almes Houses.

A Marchaunte, that longe tyme
   hadde bene in straunge landis,
Returned to his contrey,
   whiche in Europe standes.   208

A merchant returning to his country

And in his returne,
   hys waye laye to passe
By a Spittlehouse, no farre from
   where his dwelling was.   212

had to pass an hospital,

He loked for this hospitall,
   but none coulde he se ;
For a lordely house was builte
   where the hospitall should be. 216

but in its place he found a lordly house.

Good Lorde (sayd this marchaunt)
   is my contrey so wealthy,
That the verye beggers houses
   be builte so gorgiouslye ?   220

[leaf 8, back]

"Is the country so rich that beggars' houses are so fine ?"

Than, by the waye syde,
   hym chaunced to se

He soon saw a beggar, who told him they were all turned out.

A pore manne that craued
   of hym for charitie.   224

Whye (quod thys Marchaunt)
   what meaneth thys thynge?

Do ye begge by the waye,
   and haue a house for a kyng?   228

Alas! syr (quod the pore man)
   we are all turned oute,

And lye and dye in corners,
   here and there aboute.   232

Rich men had bought the place.

Men of greate riches
   haue bought our dwellinge place,

And whan we craue of them,
   they turne awaye their face.   236

The merchant had never seen such cruelty even in Turkey.

Lorde God! (quod this marchaunt)
   in Turkye haue I bene,

Yet emonge those heathen
   none such crueltie haue I sene.   240

[leaf 9]

The vengeaunce of God
   muste fall, no remedye,

Vpon these wicked men,
   and that verye shortelye.   244

Of Baylife Arrantes.

A Bailiff of the West Country, in serving his writs,

A Baylife there was
   in the weste contrey,

That dyd as they do
   in all quarters, men saye.   248

He serued with one wryte
   an whole score or tweyne,

excused those who bribed him.

And toke in hand to excuse them,
   hauinge pence for his payne.   252

And when he should warne a guest
   in sessions to appeare,
He woulde surely warne them
   that woulde make hym no cheare;   256
And then take a bribe
   to make answere for them.

He was sure to warn those who did not pay him, but only said "ahem!" to his friends.

But when he mette his frendes,
   than woulde he saye but, hem;   260
But such as had no cheare,
   nor money to paye,
Were sure to trudge
   to the sessions alwaye.   264

[leaf 9, back]
The baylefes had lande.
You must give him something—

Ye must geue him some thynge,
   to sowe his hadlande,
Or else ye can haue
   no fauoure at his hande.   268
Some puddyngis, or baken,
   or chese for to eate,

puddings, bacon, cheese, barley, malt, wheat,

A bushell of barley,
   some malt, or some wheate;   272
His hadland is good grownd,
   and beareth all thynge,
Be it baken or beffe,
   stockefyshe or lynge.   276

beef, or fish.

Thus pore men are pold
   And pyld to the bare,
By such as shoulde serue them,
   to kepe them from care.   280

Thus the poor are robbed by those who should serve them.

Of Bawdes.

THe bawdes of the stues
   be turned all out;
But some think they inhabit
   al England through out.   284

Bawds are turned out of the stews,

L

[leaf 10]
but they may be
found in taverns,
if officers would
seek them.

In tauerns and tiplyng houses
  many myght be founde,
If officers would make serch
  but as they are bounde.   288
Well, let them take heede,
  I wyll say no more ;
But when God reuengeth,
  he punisheth sore.   292

It is horrible to
fall into the
Lord's hands.

An horrible thynge
  it is, for to fall

Hebr. [x.]

Into that Lordis handis,
  that is eternall.   296

Of Beggers.

THe beggars, whome nede
  compelleth to craue.

Beggars whom
need compels
ought to have
relief,

Ought at our hauuis
  some reliefe to haue ;   300
But such as do counterfayt,
  haueynge theyr strength

but sham ones
should labour,

To labour if they luste,
  beyng knowne at the length,   304
Ought to be constrayned
  to worcke what they can,

[leaf 10, back]

And lyue on theyr laboures,

as befits Chris-
tians.

  as besemeth a Christyan ;   308
And if they refuse
  to worcke for theyr meate,

2 *Thess.*[1] 3.
If they refuse,
let them fast.

Then ought they to faste,
  as not worthy to eate.   312
And such as be sore,
  and wyll not be healed,

The sick ought to
be cared for.

Oughte not in any case
  to be charished.   316

[1] Orig. 1 Tim.

I heard of two beggars

    that vnder an hedge sate,

Who dyd wyth longe talke

    theyr matters debate.   320

They had boeth sore legges,

    most lothsome to se ;

Al rawe from the fote

    welmost to the knee.   324

" My legge," quod the one,

    " I thank God, is fayre."

" So is myne," (quod the other)

    " in a colde ayre ;   328

For then it loketh rawe,

    and as redde as any bloud,

I woulde not haue it healed,

    for any worldis good ;   332

For were it once whole,

    my lyuinge were gone,

And for a sturdye begger

    I shoulde be take anone.   336

No manne woulde pittye me,

    but for my sore legge ;

Wherfore, if it were whole,

    I might in vaine begge.   340

I shoulde be constrained

    to laboure and sweate,

And perhaps sometime

    wyth schourges be beate."   344

" Well " (sayde the tother)

    " lette vs take hede therefore,

That we let them not heale,

    but kepe them styll sore."   348

An other thynge I hearde

    of a begger that was lame,

Muche like one of these,

    if it were not the same ;   352

Of twoe beggars.

Two beggars sat talking under a hedge.

"My leg is fair," said one;

" so is mine," said the other, "in a cold air, for then it looks raw.

[leaf 11]

If it were healed my living were gone,

and I should have to work."

" Let us be careful," said the other, " to keep 'em sore."

Another beggar

Who, syttinge by the fire,
  wyth the cuppe in his hande,

Began to wonder whan
  he shoulde be a good husbande.   356

"I shall neuer thriue"
  (quod this begar) "I wene;

For I gate but .xvi. d. to daye,
  and haue spente eyghtene.   360

Well, let the worlde wagge,
  we muste neades haue drynke;

Go fyll me thys quarte pot,
  full to the brynke.   364

The tonge muste haue bastynge,
  it wyll the better wagge,

To pull a Goddes penye
  out of a churles bagge."   368

Yet cesse not to gyue to all,
  wythoute anye regarde;

Thoughe the beggers be wicked,
  thou shalte haue thy rewarde.   372

Of Bearbaytynge.

WHat follye is thys,
    to kepe wyth daunger,
    A greate mastyfe dogge
  and a foule ouglye beare?   376

And to thys onelye ende,
  to se them two fyght,

Wyth terrible tearynge,
  a full ouglye syght.   380

And yet me thynke those men
  be mooste foles of all,

Whose store of money
  is but verye smale,   384

And yet euerye Sondaye
   they will surelye spende
One penye or two,
   the bearwardes lyuyng to mende.   388 *and yet give to the bearward every Sunday.*
At Paryse garden, eche Sundaye   *Parise garden.*
   a man shall not fayle
To fynde two or thre hundredes,
   for the bearwardes vaile.   392
One halpenye a piece   *They give him a halfpenny, and perhaps that is all they have.*
   they vse for to giue,
When some haue no more
   in their purse, I belieue.   396
Well, at the laste daye,
   theyr conscience wyll declare
That the pore ought to haue   *The poor ought to have*
   all that they maye spare.   400 *what we can spare.*
For God hath commaunded,   [leaf 12, back]
   that what we maye spare   *Eccles.*[1] 4.
Be geuen to the pore,
   that be full of care.   404
If you giue it, therefore,
   to se a beare fyght,
Be ye sure Goddes curse
   wyl vpon you lyght.   408

Of Brawlers.

A Brawler, that loueth *
   to breake the kinges peace,   *A brawler is like a cur*
And seke his owne sorowe,
   his fansye to please,   412
Is lyke a curre dogge,
   that setteth vpon   *that sets upon a mastiff,*
Eche mastyfe and hounde
   that he may light on.   416

[1] Ecclesiasticus.

He getteth hym hatered
of euerye manne ;

And meteth with his maister
euer nowe and than.   420

To hurte other menne,
he taketh greate payne ;

He turneth no manne

to profite or gayne ;   424

Except it be the surgian,
or the armore,

The baylife, the constable,
or the jayler.   428

This is a worthye membre
in a commune wealthe,

That to worcke other wo
will lose his owne health.   432

What other men will iudge,
I can not tell ;

But, if he scape Tiburne,
I thinke he wyll hange in hell.   436

Of Blasphemous Swerers

THe sonne of Syrach
    wryteth playhelye
Of suche menne as do
sweare blasphemouselye.   440

" The manne that sweareth muche
shall be fylled," sayeth he,
" Wyth all wicked maners,
and iniquitie.   444

In the house of that manne

the plage shall not cease ;
He shalbe styll plaged
either more or les."   448

Christe byddeth all his
  affirme and denie.

Christ told us to
say yea and nay.

Wyth yea, yea ; nay, nay ;
  affirmyng no lye.　452
" Whatsoeuer ye ad more " (saith he)
  "cometh of iuell,
And is of the wycked
  suggestion of the deuyll."　456
But we can not talke
  wythouten othes plentye.

But we can't talk
wi .out oaths.

Some sweare by Gods nayles,
  hys herte, and his bodye ;　460
And some sweare [by] his fleshe,
  his bloude, and hys fote ;

Some swear by
God's blood,

And some by hys guttes,
  hys lyfe, and herte rote.　464
Some other woulde seme
  all sweryng to refrayne,
And they inuent idle othes,
  such is theyr idle brayne :—　468
By cocke and by pye,
  and by the goose wyng ;

some by cock and
pye,
  [leaf 14

By the crosse of the mouse fote,
  and by saynte Chyckyn.　472
And some sweare by the Diuell,
  such is theyr blyndenes ;

Math. v.
some by the
devil.

Not knowyng that they call
  these thynges to wytnes,　476
Of their consciences, in that
  they affirme or denye.
So boeth sortes commit
  Moste abhominable blasphemie.　480

They all commit
blasphemy.

Of the Colier of Croydon.

A collier at Croydon might have been a knight,

IT is sayde, that in Croydon
    there dyd sometyme dwell
A Colier, that dyd
    all other Coliers excell.   484
For his riches thys Colier
    myght haue bene a knight ;

but he would not.

But in the order of knighthode
    he hadde no delyght.   488

It would be well if knights cared no more for coaling than this collier did for knighting,
[leaf 14, back]

Woulde God all our knightes
    dyd minde colinge no more,
Than this Colier dyd knyghtyng,
    as is sayde before !   492
For when none but pore Colyars
    dyd wyth coles mell,
At a reasonable price,
    they dyd theyr coles sell ;   496

for since they have sold coals we have paid more and had less.

But sence oure Knyght Colyars
    haue had the fyrste sale,
We haue payed much money
    and had fewe sackes to tale.   500
A lode that of late yeres
    for a royall was solde,
wyll coste nowe .xvi. s.
    of syluer or golde.   504
God graunt these men grace
    theyr pollyng to refrayne,
Or els bryng them backe
    to theyr olde state agayne.   508

Men think the Croydon Collier is cousin to the collier of hell.

And especially the Colyar
    that at Croydon doth sell ;
For men thyncke he is cosen
    to the Colyar of Hell.   512

Of Commotionars.

Wнen the bodye is vexed,
    through humors corrupted,
    To restore it to helth
those humours muste be purged.   516
For if they remayne,
    they wyll styll encrease
Euery daye, more and more,
    and augment the disease ;   520
So that in short tyme
    the body muste decaye,
Except God geue health
    by some other waye.   524
Euen so doth it fare
    by the weale publyke,
Whych chaunceth to be often
    diseased and sycke,   528
Through the mischenouse malice
    of such men as be
Desyrouse to breake
    the publyke unitie.   532
Eche publyke bodye
    must be purged therfore,
Of these rotten humours,
    as is sayed before.   536
Els wyll it decay,
    as do the bodyes naturall,
When rotten humours haue
    infected them ouer all.   540
But if the publyke bodye
    can not be purged well,
By force of purgation,
    as phisickes rules do tell :   544
When bodyes be weake,
    and so lowe brought,

Side notes:

[leaf 15]
When ill humours corrupt the body

it must decay, except God give health.

So it is with the Commonwealth, which is often diseased.

The public body must be purged of its humours,

[leaf 15, back]
else it will decay.

If it cannot be purged,

That by purgation,
   no health can be wroght :   548
Then must there be sought

some easier way
must be found to
kill these hu-
mours.

   some easyar waye,
To kyl *the* strength of those humors :
   thus doth phisicke saye.   552
When the swerde wyl not helpe
   in the common wealth,
To purge it of Commotionars
   and bryng it to health :   556
Then must discrete counsell
   fynde wayes to kyll
The powr of those rebelles,
   and let them of theyr wyll.   560

[leaf 16]

And that must be by cherishyng

Natural humours,
that is, true sub-
jects, must be
cherished.

   the humours naturall,
And by quickenyng agayne
   of the spirites vitall ;   564
Whych, in the commune wealth,
   are the subiectes trew,
That do alwaye study
   sedition to eschew.   568

When these are
strong " commo-
tioners " cannot
continue.

When these men, through cherishing,
   do growe and be strong,
Then can no Commotionars
   continew long.   572
For as, when the strength
   of ill humours is kylled,
In a naturall bodye
   they be sone consumed,   576

When they see
that they cannot
do what they
wish they will
soon vanish.

Or made of iuell good,
   as it is playne to se :
So wyll it bytyde
   of such men as be,   580
In the Commune wealth,
   geuen vnto sedition,

When they se they can not
   finyshe theyr intention.   584
And what is their power,   [leaf 16, back]
   but the people ignoraunte,   Their power lies
                                      in the ignorance
Whom thei do abuse   of the people.
   by their counselles malignaunt ?   588
When the hertes of the people
   be wonne to their prince,
Than can no Commotioners
   do hurte in hys prouince.   592
If this wyll not help,   If the people are
   than God wyll take cure,   loyal seditious
                                      men can do no
And destroy these Commosioncrs,   harm.
   we may be right sure :   596
Excepte the tyme be come
   that the bodye muste dye ;
For than there canne be found
   no maner remedy.   600
God graunte that our synne   God grant that
   haue not broughte vs so lowe,   we be not past
That we be paste cure :   cure.
   God onelye doeth thys knowe ;   604
And I truste to se healthe agayne,
   if the finall ende
Be not nowe nere at hande ;
   whyche the Lorde shortelye sende.   608

Of Commen Drunkardes.   [leaf 17]

ESaye lamenteth,   Isaiah laments
   and sayeth, "oute, alas !   Esaye .v.
Muche wo shall betide you,
   that do youre tyme passe   612
In eatinge and drinckynge,
   from morninge to nighte,

Til none of your membres
 canne do his office righte.   616

Woe be to you," sayeth he,

because the Jews
rose up early to
drink like beasts.
 " that do so earlye rise,

To fyll your selues wyth drincke
 in suche beastelye wise."   620

But if he were nowe liuyng,
 and sawe this worldes state,

If he saw our
drunkards he
would see they
did not rise
early, but sat up
late.
He wold saye this of our drunkards,
 that sytte vp so late.   624

For fewe of oure drunckardes
 do vse to rise earelye ;

But muche of the nighte
 they wyll drincke lustelye. 628

i. Cor. v.¹
Well, Sainte Paule doeth warne
 all that be of pure mynde,

To auoide drunckardes company,

[leaf 17, back]
 where so euer they do them finde. 632

Paul tells us not
to eat or drink
with drunkards,
So ye neyther eate nor drincke
 wyth suche menne, sayeth he,

That be geuen to drinkinge,
 what so euer they be.   636

but, alas! our
curates excel their
parishioners in
drinking.
But, alas ! manye curates,
 that shoulde vs thys tell, ·

Do all their parishioners
 in drynckyng excell.   640

Of Commune Liars.

Solomon says a
liar slays the soul.
Sapi. i.
SOlomon the sage,
 in Sapience doeth saye,

That the mouthe that lyeth
 doeth the verye soule sleye. 644

If the murderer of bodies
 be worthye to dye,

     ¹ Orig. i.

The murderer of soules
   shoulde not escape, trowe I.   648
For as the soule doeth
   the bodye excell,
So is his treaspace greater,
   that doeth the soule quell.   652
But lyars (alas !)
   are nowe muche set by,
And thought to be menne
   in a maner necessarie   656
To be entertayned
   of eche noble manne,
Who are muche delighted
   wyth lyes nowe and than.   660
But this delite will be sorowe,
   I feare me, at the laste ;
Whan the liar, for hys liynge,
   into paynes shall be caste.   664

Liars are not punished,

but are thought much of,

[leaf 18]

and are thought necessary to noblemen.

This delight in lies will not last.

Of Dicears.

EMonge wyttye saiynges,
   this precept I finde,
To auoid and fle dice (mi son)
   haue euer in mynde.   668
For diceynge hath brought many
   wealthye menne to care ;
And manye ryche heyre
   it hath made full bare.   672
Some menne it hath sette vp,
   I wyll not denye,
And brought to more worship,
   than they be worthye.   676
God knoweth to what ende
   he suffereth thys thing ;

Cato advised to flee dice-playing,

Cato.

which has stripped many.

It has set up some,

[leaf 19, back]

perhaps to re-
ward them in
hell.

Perchaunce to rewarde them
   wyth hel at their endynge.   680
For doubtlesse those goodes
   are gotten amisse,
That are gotten from him
   that prodigall is ;   684

At dice both
intend to get
others' goods.

And especially at the dyce,
   where boeth do intende
To get others goods,
   or else hys owne to spende.   688
Nowe if prodigalitye
   or couetise be vyce,
He cannot but offend
   that playeth at the dyce.   692
For be they two or mo,
   thys thyng is certayne,

Prodigality and
covetousness
reign in both.

Prodigalytie and couetise
   do in them all raygne.   696
Besyde the wycked othes,
   and the tyme myspent,
Wherof they thincke they nede not
   them selues to repent.   700

[leaf 19]

But thys I dare saye,

If dicing is not
sinful,

   that though dyceyng were no sin,
Nor the goodis mysgoten,
   that men do ther at wynne ;   704

the oaths and
the misspent
time will be the
condemnation of
the players.

Yet the othes that they swere,
   and the tyme myspent,
Shall be theyr dammacion,
   vnlesse they repent.   708
Leaue of your vayne dyceyng,
   ye dycers, therefore,
For vnlesse ye repent,
   God hath vengeaunce in store ;   712
And when ye thynke least,
   then wyl he pour it oute,

And make you to stoupe,

he ye neuer so stoute.

716

God will make
them stoop un-
less they repent.

Of Double Benificed Men.

THe kynge of that realme,

    where iustice doeth reygne,

Perused olde statutis,

    that in bokis remayne.   720

And as he turned the boke,

    him chaunced to se,

That such as haue benifices

    shoulde resident be ;   724

And haue theyr abydyng,

    whyles theyr lyfe shoulde endure,

Emong them, ouer whome

    God hath geuen them cure.   728

Then sayed he to him selfe,

    " I thyncke well there is

No lawe in thys realme

    worse obserued then this.   732

Yet can there nothynge

    My flocke more decaye,

Then when hyrelynges suffer

    My shepe go astraye."   736

Then called he his councell

    And tolde them his mynde,

And wylled that they shoulde

    some remedy fynde.   740

Whoe, wyth good aduice,

    agreed on this thyng,

That visitours should be sent,

    wyth the powre of the kyng,   744

To punyshe all such

    as herein dyd offende,

A certain king
looked over some
statutes which
said beneficed
men should be
resident.

[leaf 19, back]

He thought no
law was so little
observed.

He called his
Council,

and sent visitors
to punish all that
should disobey
this law.

[leaf 20]

Vnlesse they were founde
thorowe wyllynge to amende.   748

The visitors
found only one
priest who would
surrender none.
Osee .iiii.

These visitours found many stout
priestes, but chicflye one
That hadde sondrye benifices,
but woulde surrender none.   752
Than was this stoute felowe
brought to the kynge,
Who sayde vnto hym,
    " Syr, howe chaunceth this thing?   756
Wyl ye transegresse my lawes?
    and than disobeye

He was brought
to the king, and
pleaded the royal
" grant of a
plurality,"

Menne hauing my power?
    Syr, what can you saye?"   760
    " If it mai like your grace," (quod he)
    " loe, heare is to se;
Your seale at a graunte
    of a pluralitie."   764
    " Well," saide the kinge than,
    " I repente me of all yll;
But tell me, maister doctoure,
    wil you haue your benifices styll?"   768

and said if he had
right he must
keep them for his
lifetime.
[leaf 20, back]

    " If your grace do me ryghte," (q*uod* he)
    " I must haue them my life tyme."
    " So shalt thou," (quod the kynge)
    " for to morow by pryme,   772
God wyllynge, thy body
    shalbe diuided, and sent,
To ech benifice a piece,
    to make the resident.   776
Away wyth hym" (quod the kyng)
    " and let al thyngis be done,

" So shalt thou;
for to-morrow
thy body shall be
divided, and part
sent to each
benefice,

As I haue geuen sentence,
    to morow ere none.   780
For syth thou arte a stout[1] priest,
    an example thou shalt be,
            [1] stout in original.

That all stouburne priestes
  may take warnyng by the."

that all may take
warning."

784

Of the Exchecker.

IN the weste parte of Europe
  there was sometyme a kynge,
That had a court for receyte
  of money to him belongeing.

*In the West a
king had a court
for the receipt of
money.*

788

But the ministers of that court
  dyd longe, and many a daye,
Take brybes to bare *with* suche me*n*
  as should forfaytis pay.

*The officers took
bribes.*

792

At the laste, to the Kyng
  this theyr falshode was tolde,
By suche as about hym,
  were faythfull and bolde.

[leaf 21]

796

Then dyd the Kyng sende
  for these ministers ill,
And layde all theyr faltes
  before them in a byll.

*When the king
heard of it he
sent for them.*

800

Then were they abashed,
  and had nought to saye,
But cryed for hys perdon;
  but he bade, "Awaye;

*They cried for
mercy, but he
sent them away*

804

Ye haue borne wyth theues,
  and haue robbed me,
And suffered my people
  impoueryshed to be.

808

No statute coulde cause
  thoffendars to emende,
Because you bare wyth them,
  when they dyd offende.

812

Awaye wyth them all,
  laye them in prisone,

*to prison to await
judgment.*

5

Tyll we haue determined,
  what shall wyth them be done."   816

What iudgment they had
  I haue not hearde yet ;

But well I wot they deserued
  a Tiburne typpet.   820

   .

Of Flaterars.

A Flatterynge frende
    is worse then a foe ;
For a frende is betrusted,
  when the other is not so.   824

Of an open enimie,
  a man may be ware ;
When the flatteryng frend
  wyl worcke men much care.   828

For if Abner had knowne
  what was in Ioabs harte,
I do not doubt but he would
  haue out of his waye sterte ;   832
Or, at the leaste, he would not
  haue admitted hym so ny

As to be embraced of hym,
  and on his dagger to dye.   836
Wherefore I aduertise
  al men to be ware

Of all flatterynge frendis,
  that bring men to care.   840

As for open ennimies,
  trust them if ye wyll ;
I can not forbyd you
  to admyt your owne yll.   844
Woulde God all men woulde
  such flatterars trye,

As hange at theyr elbowes,
   to get some what therby.   848

But (alas !) nowe adayes,
   men of honour do promote

Now-a-days men of honour promote flatterers,

Many a false flatterynge
   and lewde harlot ;   852

Whych thynge may at the lengthe
   be theyr owne decaye ;

For if the wynde turne,
   the flatterars wyll awaye.   856

who, if the wind turns, will leave them.

The swallowe in sommer
   wyll in your house dwell ;

But when wynter is commynge,
   she wyll saye farewell.   860

as the swallow leaves man in winter,

And when the short dayes
   begyn to be colde,

Robinredbrest wil come home to ye,
   and be very bolde ;   864

[leaf 22, back] and the robin in the summer.

But when summer returneth,
   and bushes wax grene,

then Robyn your man
   wyll no more be sene.   868

So some of your flattera[r]s
   wyll in prosperitie,

be of your householde,
   and of your family ;   872

Some flatterers will remain while you are prosperous :

And some other wyl,
   when nede doth them payne,

Sue to do you seruice,
   tyll they be welthy agayne.   876

others will seek you when they are poor.

Of Foles.

THe Preachar sayeth thus,
   "a pore wytty ladde

A witty lad is better than a *Eccle. iiii.* foolish old king.

is better then an olde Kynge,
whose wytte is but badde." 880
The wyse man in pouertie
is ryght honourable,
Whan the fole in his ryches,
is worthy a bable. 884

Some foles there be of nature,
that vnderstande nought;
Some other vnderstand thynges,
but haue euer in theyr thought, 888

That they them selues be wysest;
whych folly passeth all,
And doeth soneste appeare,
as well in greate as small. 892
These foles wyll not heare
any mans reade or counsell,
And what soeuer they them selfe do,
is excedyng well; 896
But other mens doynges
they wyll euer dypreuse,

For other can do nought
that may theyr mynde please. 900
And, further, they thyncke
it becometh them well,
in euery mans matter
them selfe to entermel. 904
And when they come in place
where is any talke,

No man shal fynde a tyme to speake,
so faste theyr tonges shal walke. 908

Of theyr owne dedis and goodes,
they wyll bragge and boaste,
And declare all theyr mishaps,
and what they haue loste. 912

If ye tell them of theyr fautes,
then wyll they nedes fyght:

Ye must sayô as they saye,
　Be it wroungo or ryght.　　　916

In fine, ye must prayse them,
　and sette forth theyr fame ;

You must praise them.

And what soeuer they do,
　you may them not blame.　　920

If ye tell them of knowledge,
　they saye they lacke none,

And wyshe they had lesse,
　and then they make mone,　　924

For the losso of vayne toyes,
　wherin they delyte ;

And then, if ye reasone farre,
　beware, they wyll fyght.　　928

If you reason with them, they will fight. All wise men shun them.

All wise men, take hede,
　and shunne theyr companye,

For of all other men,
　they are most vngodly.　　932

Of Forestallars.

[leaf 24]

THe fryses of Walis
　　to Brystowe are brought;

Welsh friezes are bought before they are woven.

But before thei were wouen,
　in Walis they are bought ;　　936

So that nowe we do paye
　foure grotes, or els more,

For the fryse[1] we haue bought
　for eyght pens heretofore.　　940

And some saye the woule
　is bought ere it do growe,

Some say the wool is bought before it is grown.

And the corne long before
　it come in the mowe.　　944

And one thyng there is
　that hurteth moste of all ;

　　　　[1] Orig. " fryfe "

Reuersions
of farms and
benefices are
bought.

Reuersions of fermes are bought
  long ere they fall.   948
And ryght so are benifices
  in euery coaste,
So that persons and vicars
  kepe neyther sodde nor roste.   952
The pore of the paryshe,
  whome the person shoulde fede,
Can haue nought of oure tythis,

[leaf 24, back]

  to sucuoure theyr nede.   956
Reuersions of fermes
  are bought on ech syde ;

Old tenants must
pay well if they
would remain.

And the olde tenant must pay well,
  if he wyll a byde.   960
And where the father payde a peny,
  and a capon or twayne,
The sonne muste paye ten pownde :
  [t]his passeth my brayne.   964
Well, let thes forestallars
  repent them bytyme,

The clerk of the
market will
punish these
engrossers and
forestallers.

Leste the clarke of the market
  be wyth them ere pryme.   968
For he, when he cometh,
  wyll punysh them all,
That do any nedeful thynge
  ingrose or forestall.   972
For well I wotte thys,

When he went
away his servant
told us not to
seek our own
profit.

i. Cor. x.

  when he went laste awaye,
He sent vs his seruaunt,
  and thus dyd he saye.   976
Se that emong you
  none seke his owne gayne,
But profyte ech other

[leaf 25]

  wyth trauayle and payne.   980

Of Godlesse Men.

HOlye Dauid, that was
  boeth propheth and kinge,
Sawe in hys tyme
  (as appeareth by hys wrytynge)
That in those dayes
  there were men of wycked hert,
That dyd all godlye wayes
  vtterlye peruerte.
And so there are nowe,
  the pitye is the more,
That lyue more carnalye
  than euer men[2] dyd before.
These men (sayeth kinge Dauid)
  in their hertes do saye,
Surelye there is no God,
  let vs take our owne waye.
Thus iudged kyng Dauid,
  and that for good skyll,
Bicause he sawe their worckes,
  were wycked and euyll.
They are (sayeth he) corrupt,
  and nought in all theyr wayes,
Not one doeth good ;
  and therfore he sayes,
That they thincke there is no God,
  theyr worckis do declare,
For to do the thynge that good is
  they haue no maner care.
But what would Dauid saye,
  if he were in these dayes,
When men wyl do ill,
  and iustifie theyr yl weyes ?

David in his time
saw wicked men,

984 *Psalm xiv.*[1]

who perverted
godly ways.

988

So now there are
men more carnal
than ever.

992

996

1000

[leaf 25, back]

1004

and their deeds
declare it.

1008

What would
David say now ?

1012

[1] Orig. i. [2] Repeated in orig.

They leaue the good vndone,
   and do that yll is;
And then they call that yll good—
   what woulde Dauid saye to this?   1016
I know not what Dauid
   would saye in this case;

But I knowe that good Esay
   doeth cursse them apase.   1020
Woe! sayth this prophete,
   to them that do call
That thyng good that euell is.
   but this is not all: 1024
He sayeth woe to them

   that call dearckenes lyght,
Preferryng theyr fansey
   before the worde of myght.   1028

If they fynde a thynge wrytten
   in Paul, Luke, or John,
Or any other scripture,

   they wyll therof none,   1032
Except they may easily
   perceyue and se
That, wyth theyr fleshly fansey,
   they may make it agre.   1036
All other textis of scripture
   they wyll not stycke to deny;
Yea, some of them wyll
   God and his scripture defie,   1040
And say they wyl make meric here,
   for when they be gone

They can haue no ioye,
   for soule they haue none.   1044
If these menne be not godles,
   muche meruell haue I.

Well, the cause is the Lordes,
   lette hym and them trye.   1048

I knowe at the laste,
    they shall fynde him to strong :
The daye of his vengeaunce
    wyll not tarye long.   1052

[leaf 26, back]
and they will find
Him strong.

Of Idle Persons.

IDlenes hath ben cause
    of much wyckednes,
As Ecclesiasticus
    doeth playnely wytnes,   1056
Idle persons, therfore,
    can not be all cleare,
As by the storie of Sodome,
    it doeth well appeare.   1060
But that we may come nere
    to our owne age,
The idlenes of abbays
    made them outrage.   1064
Yet let vs come neare,
    euen to the tyme present,
And se what myschyfe
    Idle persons do inuent ;   1068
What conspiracies haue ben wroght,
    Wythin this lyttle whyle,
By idle men that dyd
    the commons begyle ;   1072
And what haue idle men
    alwaye practised,
To breake the peace of prynces,
    that they myght be hyered.   1076
I wyll not saye what
    the idlenes of priestes hath done,
Nor yet the idlenes
    of seruauntis in London.   1080

Idleness causes
much wickedness,

Eccles. 33.

as was seen in
Sodom,

and the abbeys.

Now idle persons
hatch con-
spiracies.

[leaf 27]

What the idleness
of priests and
servants in Lon-
don has done,

Let eueri man search
   his owne houshold well,
And whether the thynge
   be true that I tell.   1084
Yea, what abuse dyd euer
   emonge the people rayne,
But the same dyd fyrst sprynge
   out of an idle brayn?   1088

Idlenes, therfore,
   maye ryghte well be named
The gate of all mischiefe
   that euer was framed.   1092

Ye masters and fathers, therfore,
   that feare God omnipotent,
Kepe youre families,

   leaste ye be shente;   1096
For if thorowe their idlenes
   they fall into outrage,
Your iudgemente shall be strayght,

   for they are committed to your charg.   1100
Kepe them, therfore, styll occupied,
   in doynge youre busines,
Or els in readynge or hearynge
   some bokes of godlines.   1104

And woulde God the maiestrates
   woulde se men set a-worke,
And that within thys realme
   none were suffered to lurke.   1108

This realme hath thre commoditie
   woule, tynne, and leade,
Which being wrought within the realme,
   eche man might get his bread.   1112

¶ Of Inuenters of Straunge Newes.

SOme men do delite
   straunge newes to inuente,

Of this mannes doynge,
  and that mannes intente ;   1116
What is done in Fraunce,   of Foreign parts,
  and in the Emperours lande ;   [leaf 28]
And what thyng the Scottes
  do nowe take in hande ;   1120
What the Kynge and his counsell,
  do intende to do ;
Though for the most parte   which for the
  it be nothynge so.   1124   most part is
                                                     untrue.
Such men cause the people,
  that els woulde be styll,
To murmour and grudge,   Such men make
  whych thyng is very ill.   1128   the people
                                                     murmur.
Yea, sometyme they cause   *We sawe the*
  the people to ryse,   *experience of*
                                                     thys of late.
And assemble them selfe
  in most wycked wyse.   1132
In Plato hys common wealth,   Plato expelled all
  such men shoulde not dwell,   poets and orators
                                                     from his com-
For poetes and oratoures   monwealth.
  he dyd expell.   1136
Oh ! that these newes bryngars
  had for theyr rewarde,
Newe halters of hemppe,   They want new
  to sette them forwarde !   halters.
                                             1140

¶ Of Laye Men that take Tithes,   [leaf 28, back]
  and Priests that vse theyr Ti-
    t[h]es priuatly.

WHan Iustice began   When Justice
     in iudgment to syt,   began to sit in
                                                     judgment
To punysh all such men
  as dyd fautes commit ;   1144

Then was there a man
    before hyr accused,

a man was
accused of using
tithes for private
purposes

For tythes that he toke,
    and priuately vsed.   1148

When dewe proufe was had,
    and the thyng manifeste,

The wyttnesses sworne,
    and the treaspace confeste ;   1152

Then gaue the iudge iudgement
    and these wordes he spake :—

He was deprived
of all his goods,

" Se that from this caytyfe
    ye do all his goodes take ;   1156

For seynge he made that priuate,
    that commune shoulde be,

He shall haue this iustice,
    by the iudgment of me.   1160

Those pore men, that by the tithes

[leaf 29]

    shoulde be releued,

which were
divided among
the poor,

Shal haue all his goodes
    emonge them diuided.   1164

Iacob ii.

And because he shewed no mercie,
    no mercie shall he haue.

and then he was
hanged.

The sentence is geuen,
    go hange vp the slaue."   1168

Of Leasemongars.

A leasemonger's
conscience
pricked him
when he thought
he was a-dying.

O F late a leasemongar
    of London laye sycke,

And thynckyng to dye,
    his conscience dyd him pricke.   1172

Wherefore he sayde thus
    wyth hym selfe secretly,

So he sent for a
preacher.

" I wyll sende for a preachar,
    to knowe what remedy."   1176

But whilse he thus laye,
 he fell in a sloumber,
and sawe in his dreame
 pore folke a greate number,   1180
Whoe sayde they had learned thys
 at the preachars hande,
To paye all wyth patience,
 that theyr landlordes demaunde. 1184
For they for theyr sufferaunce,
 in such oppression,
Are promised rewarde
 in the resurrection.   1188
Where such men as take leases
 them selues to aduaunce,
Are sure to haue hell
 by ryght inheritaunce.   1192

Then he dreamed that poor folks said they had learned to pay what landlords demanded,

[leaf 29, back]

because they would be rewarded in the resurrection, but leasemongers are sure of hell.

Of Marchauntes.

IF Marchauntes wold medle
 wyth marchaundice onely,
And leaue fermes to such men,
 as muste lyue thereby ;   1196
Then were they moste worthy
 to be had in price,
As men that prouide vs
 of all kyndes marchaundice.   1200
But syth they take fermes,
 to let them out agayne,
To such men as muste haue them,
 though it be to theyr payn :   1204
And to leauye greate fines,
 or to ouer the rent,
And do purchayse greate landes,
 for the same intent :   1208

If merchants would let farms alone it would be well.

But they take them and let them out again, raising the rents.

[leaf 30]

They are un-
profitable.

We muste nedes cal them
    membres vnprofitable,
As men that woulde make
    all the Realme miserable.   1212
Howe they leaue theyr trade,

They also lend
money to young
merchants.

    and lende oute theyr money,
To yonge marchaunte men,
    for greate vsurie ;   1216
Whereby some yonge men
    are dreuen to leaue all,
And do into moste extreme
    pouertie fall,   1220
It greueth me to wryte.

What is the
remedy ?

    but what remedy ?
They muste heare theyr faute,
    syth they be so greedye.   1224
And thus I saye to them,
    and trewe they shall it fynde,

The Lord will
have them in
mind,

The Lorde wyll haue all
    theyr iuell doynges in mynde.   1228
And at the laste daye,
    when they shall aryse,

[leaf 30, back]

All shall be layed playne
    before theyr owne eyes,   1232

and they will get
judgment without
mercy.

Where iudgemente shall be geuen,
    as Saynte Iames doeth wytnes,

Iacob .ii.

Wythoute all mercye
    to suche as be merciles   1236

Of Men that haue Diuers Offices.

In Rome ambi-
tion was punished
with exile,

WHan the Citye of Rome
    was ruled aryght,
    As aunciente autours
do recorde and wryte   1240

Ambition was punished
  wyth vtter exile ;
Yet were there some that dyd
  venter some whyle.   1244

But we reade not of anye
  that euer wente aboute,
To haue two offices at once,
  were they neuer so stoute.   1248

But, alas ! in this Realme,
  we counte hym not wyse,
That seketh not by all meanes
  that he canne deuise,   1252

To take offices togither,
  wythoute anye staye.

But Christe shal saie to these menne
  at the laste daye,   256

Geue accounts of your baliwickes,
  ye mene wythout grace,
Ye that soughte to be rulers
  in euerye place,   1260

Geue accountes of your baliwike,
  for come is the daye
That ye muste leaue youre offices,
  and walke your fathers waye.   1264

Side notes:
yet some ventured to return.
But none seem to have had two offices at once, as they do here.
[leaf 31]
At the last day Christ will demand an account of your stewardship. Luke .xvi.

Of Nice Wyues.

THe sonne of Sirache
  of women doeth saye,
That theire nicenes & hordom
  is perceiued alwaye   1268
By there wanton lokes,
  And lyftynge vp of eyes,
And their lokinge ascoye,
  in most wanton wise.   1272

Side note:
The son of Sirach says, a woman may be known by wanton looks. Eccles. 26.

And in the same
Eccles. xi[x].
Iesus Syrach, I fynde

He also says that the walk and the [leaf 31, back] dress declare the mind.
That the gate and the garment
   do declare the mynde.   1276
If these thynges be trew,
   (as, no doubt, they be)

If so what are we to think of the London women?
What shold we thynk of *the* women
   that in London we se?   1280
For more wanton lokes,
   I dare boldely saye,
Were neuer in Iewyshe whores,
   then in London wyues thys daye.   1284

" If gait and garments show anything," our wives surpass all whores.
And if gate and garmentes
   do shewe any thynge,
Our wiues do passe their whoris
   in whorelyke deckynge.   .   1288
I thynk the abhominable
   whores of the stews
Dyd neuer more whorelyke
   attyrementes vse.   1292

Their caps are like a sow's maw;
The cappe on hyr heade
   is lyke a sowes mawe ;
Such an other facion
   I thynk neuer Iewe sawe.   1296
Then fyne geare on the forcheade,
   sette after the new trycke,
Though it coste a crowne or two,
[leaf 32]
   What then? they may not stycke.   1300

If their hair won't dye they buy new, and lay it out in tussocks,
If theyr heyre wyl not take colour,
   then must they by newe,
And laye it oute in tussockis :
   this thynge is to true.   1304

one on each side as big as a ball.
At ech syde a tussocke,
   as bygge as a ball,—
A very fayre syght
   for a fornicator bestiall.   1308

Hyr face faire paynted,
  to.make it shyne bryght,
And hyr bosome all bare,
  and most whorelyke dight. 1312

Their faces are painted, their bosoms bare.

Hyr mydle braced in,
  as smal as a wande ;
And some by wastes of wyre
  at the paste wyfes hande. 1316

Their waists are braced in,

A bumbe lyke a barrell,
  wyth whoopes at the skyrte ;

and their bums like a barrel.

Hyr shoes of such stuffe
  that may touche no dyrte ; 1320

Shoes must not touch the dirt.

Vpon hyr whyte fyngers,
  manye rynges of golde,

Rings on fingers.

Wyth suche maner stones
  as are most dearlye solde. 1324 *[leaf 32, back]*

Of all their other trifles,
  I wyll saye nothynge,
Leaste I haue but small thanckes,
  for thys my writynge. 1328

All modeste matrons
  I truste wyll take my parte,
As for nice whippets, wordes
  shall not come nye my hert. 1332

All modest matrons will, I hope, take my part.

I haue tolde them but trueth,
  let them saye what they wyll ;
I haue sayde they be whorelike,
  and so I saye styll.   _ 1336

I have said they are whorelike, and so they are.

Of Obstinate Papistes.

AN obstinate papiste,
  that was sometyme a frier,
Hadde of his friers cote
  so greate a desire, 1340

A friar so desired to wear his friar's coat

6

that he went to
Louvain to put
it on.

That he stale out of England,
   and wente to Louayne,
And gate his fryers cote
   on his foles backe agayne.   1344
A wilfull beggar

[leaf 33]

   this papist wyl be,
A fole and a fryer,
   and thus is one man thre.   1348

Would God all
the Papists were
with him !

Would God all·the papistis,
   that he lefte behynde,
Where wyth him in frye[r]s cotis
   accordyng to theyr kynde ;   1352
Or els I woulde they were
   wyth theyr father the Pope,
For whylse they be in England,
   thei do but lyue in hope.   1356

Unless they can
burn the Bible
they will despair.

And excep[t] they myght get
   the Bible boke burned,
Into dispeyre theyr hope
   wyl shortly be turned.   1360

God grant that
they may take
their natural
prince for their
head, and forsake
the Pope.

God graunte them the grace
   this hope to forsake,
And their naturall prynce
   for theyr heade to take ;   1364
Forsakinge the Pope,
   wyth al hys peltrye,
Whiche of longe tyme
   they haue sette so much by.   1368

[leaf 33, back]

Of Rente Raysers.

A man surveyed
his lands, and
let them out dear.

A Manne that had landes,
   of tenne pounde by yere,
Surueyed the same,
   and lette it out deare ;   1372

So that of tenne pounde
   he made well a score
Moe poundes by the yere
   than other dyd before.   1376
But when he was tolde
   whan daunger it was
To oppresse his tenauntes,
   he sayed he did not passe.   1380
For thys thynge, he sayde,
   full certayne he wyste,
That wyth hys owne he myghte
   alwayes do as he lyste.   1384
But immediatlye, I trowe
   thys oppressoure fyl sicke
Of a voyce that he harde,
   " geue accountes of thy baliwicke ! "   1388

Side note at lines 1376–1388: When he was told it was dangerous to oppress his tenants, he said he could do as he liked with his own.

Side note: But he soon died. *Luke* .xvi.

Of Vayne Wryters, Vaine Talkers and Vaine Hearers.

OF late, as I laye,
   and lacked my reste,
At suche time as Titan
   drewe faste to the Easte,   1392
Thys sayinge of Christe
   came into my minde,
Whyche certayne and true
   all maner menne shall fynde :—   1396
Of euerye idle worde
   ye shall geue a rekeninge ;
Be it spoken by mouthe,
   or put in wrytynge.   1400
O Lorde (thought I then)
   what case be th[e]y in,
That talke and write vaynely,
   And thinke it no synne ?   1404

Side note: [leaf 34] As I lay restless

Side note: Christ's saying about idle words came into my mind.

Side note: Math. xii.

Side note: What a case they are in who write and talk vainly !

Than slombred I a little,
and thoughte that I sawe

I thought I saw
three vain men
condemned and
punished.

Thre sortes of vayne menne
condempned by Gods lawe.   1408

The one was a wryter,
of thynges nought and vayne,

And an other a talker;
And thys was theyr payne: 1412

[leaf 34, back]
The writer's head
was opened, and
the talker stirred
his brains with
a stick;

The wryter hadde the crowne
of hys heade opened,

Whose braynes wyth a stycke
the talker styrred;   1416

while the writer
pulled the talker's
tongue out a
hand-length;

And he wyth boeth handes
drewe the talkers tonge,

So that wythout hys mouthe
it was an handefull longe.   1420

and the listener's
ears were pulled
almost up to
his eyes.

The thirde was an herkener
of fables and lyes,

Whose eares were almost
drawen vp to his eyes.   1424

Of Vnsaciable Purchasers.

A rich man rode
out, and had only
a boy with him.

A N vnreasonable ryche man
    dyd ryde by the way,

Who, for lacke of menne,
hadde wyth hym a boye.   1428

And as he paste by a pasture
most pleasaunte to se,

"Jack, I have
bought this
ground."

"Of late I haue purchasid
thys grounde, Iacke," quod he.   1432

"Marry, men
say your pur-
chase is great,
but your house-
hold small."

"Mary, maister" (quod the boye)
"men saye ouer all,

That your purchase is greate,
but your housholde is smal."   1436

" Why, Iacke" (quod this riche man)
    " what haue they to do?
Woulde they haue me to purchase
    and kepe·greate house to?"   1440
" I can not tell" (quod the boye)
    " what maketh them to brawle ;
But they saye that ye purchase
    the Deuill, his dame, and all."   1444

[leaf 35]
"Why, Jack,
would they have
me buy and keep
a great house
too?"

Luk. xiiii.
"I don't know
why they brawl—
they say you buy
the devil and his
dam."

Of Vsurars.

A Certaine man had landes,
    little thoughe it were ;
And yet wold faine haue liued
    lyke a gentleman's peare.   1448
Of thys lande he made sale,
    and toke readye golde,
And let that for double the rente
    of the lande that was solde.   1452
Than came there a broker,
    and sayde if he woulde do
As he woulde aduise hym,
    he shoulde make of one penye two.   1456
" Marye that woulde I fayne do "
    (quod this vsurer than)
" I praye the teache me
    the feat if thou can."   1460
" You shall " (sayde thys broker)
    " lende but for a monethes day,
And be sure of
    a sufficiente[1] gage alwaye,   1464
Wyth a playne bill of sale ;
    if the day be not kept,
And se that ye do
    no causis accepte.   1468

A man had a
little land, but
wanted to live
like a gentleman,
so he sold his
land, and lent the
money.

A broker came
and offered to
tell him how to
make twopence
of a penny.

[leaf 35, back]

"Lend only for a
'month's day'
with good se-
curity, and a bill
of sale.

[1] Orig. suffitience

CROWLEY.   4

6 ★

Your interest
must be a penny
for a shilling,
then at the year's
end twelve
months will give
twelve pence."

Than muste you be sure
    that your intereste be
One penye for a shyllynge,
    and thre pence for three.   1472
So by the yeres ende,
    twelue moneths geue twelue pens,
For the vse of a shyllynge.
    lo, I haue tolde you all sens."   1476
Than saide this vsurer,
    "this matter goeth well,

"This will do:
my twenty pounds
will produce four
hundred, and I
can live like a
lord."

For my twentye pounde lande,
    that I chaunced to sell,   1480
I shall haue foure hundred
    pounde rente by the yere,
To lyue lyke a Lorde,

[leaf 36]

    and make iolye chere."   1484

But a prophet
came, and told
him heaven was
no place for such
unlawful gain.

Psal. xv.

Than came there a Prophete,
    and tolde thys manne playne,
That h[e]auen is no place
    for suche vnlawefull gayne.   1488
"Why, sir" (quod this Vsurar)
    "it is my liuynge."
"Yea, sir" (quod this Prophet)
    "but it is not youre calling ;   1492

"You are to live
on £20 a year
till God shall
increase the
amount ;

You are called to liue
    after twentye pounde by yere,
And after that rate
    ye shoulde measure your chere,   1496
Tyll God did encrease you
    by his mercifull wayes,
By encreasynge youre corne,
    and youre cattell in the leyes ;   1500

and with the
increase you are
to profit all who
live near you.

Whyche encrese wyth your landes
    you are bounde to employe,
To the profite of all them
    that do dwell you bye.   1504

Ye are not borne to your selfe,
  neither maye you take
That thynge for youre owne,
  where of God did you make   1508   [leaf 36, back]
But stuarde and baylife,
  that shall yelde a rekeninge
At the Daye of Iudgmente
  for euerye thyng.   1512
And do ye not doubte,
  but then ye shall knowe,
Whether ye maye your goodes
  at youre pleasure bestowe ;   1516
And whether ye maye vse
  wayes wycked and yl,
To incraese your riches
  at your owne will.   1520
But chieflye to lende
  youre goodes to vsurie,
Is a thinge that you shall
  moste dearelye abye ;   1524
For Christe saieth in Luke
  that the heathen do so.
Take hede lest ye flytte
  frome pleasure to woe."   1528

Marginal notes:
At the Judgment you will learn whether you may do as you like *Luke xvi.* with your own.

To lend your money for usury is a thing you will suffer for. Christ says the heathen do so."

Luke .vi.

        Finis.

¶ Cum p[r]iuilegio ad imprimendum solum.

The Voyce of

the laste trumpet, blowen by the seuenth Angel (as is mentioned in the ele=
uenth of the Apocalips) callyng al estats
of men to the ryght path of theyr vocation, wherin are conteyned .xii. Lessons to
twelue scueral estats of men, which if
thei learne and folowe, al shall be
* wel, and nothing amis *
~ * ~

¶ The voyce of one criynge
in the deserte.
Luke .iii.

¶ Make redy the Lords waie, make his
pathes streight. Euery balley shalbe fyl=
led, and euery mountayne and lyttle hyl
shalbe made lowe, and thynges that be cro=
ked shalbe made streyght, & hard passa=
ges shalbe turned into plaine waies, and
all flesh shall se the hea[l]th of God.
Esaie .xl.

¶ Imprinted at London by Robert Crowley, dwellynge in Elie
rents in Holburn. Anno Do.
M D L.

¶ Cum priuilegio ad impri=
mendum solum.

The Boke to the Readar.

It pleased mine autor to geue me of nam[e]
The voice of the last trumpe (as S. Iohn doeth wryte)
Thincking therby to auoyd all the blame
That commenli chaunceth to such men as wryte   4
Plainly to such men as walk not upright :
For truth gette[t]h hatred of such as be yll,
And wil sufer nothing *that* bridleth their wil.   7

I am named the Last Trumpet

to avoid all blame.

If ought do displese you, let me bere *the* wit,
For I am tho doar of all that is done ;
I bark at your fauts, but loth I am to byt,
If by this barkyng ought myght be won :   11
And for thys intent I was firste bigonne,
That, hearing your fautes, ye myght them emende,
And reigne *with* our master Christ in the end.   14

Though I bark I am unwilling to bite.

Hearing your faults, may you amend them.

The Contents of this Boke.

The Beggars Lesson.

Whoso woulde that all thynges were well,
    And woulde hymselfe be wyth out blame,
Let hym geue eare, for I wyll tell
The waye how to performe the same.   4

    Fyrste walke in thy vocation,
And do not seke thy lotte to chaunge ;
For through wycked ambition,
Many mens fortune hath ben straynge.   8

Let those who would have all things well give ear to me.

Walk in your vocation, and don't try to change your lot.

THE BEGGARS LESSON.

If God haue layede hys hande on the,
    And made the lowe in al mens syght,
Content thiselfe *with* that degre,
And se thou walke therin upryght.   12

    If thou, I saye, be very pore,
And lacke thine health or any limme,
No doubte God hath inough in store
For the, if thou wylt truste in hym. ·   16

    If thou wylt truste in hym, I saye,
And continue in patience,
No doubt he wyll fede the alwaye
By his mercifull prouidence.   20

    Call thou on hym, and he wyll moue
The hertes of them that dwel the by,
To geue the such thynges for hys loue
As serue for thy necessitie.   24

    When Daniell was in the denne
Of Lions, haueynge nought to eate,
Abacucke was sent to him then,
With a pot of potage and meate.   28

If you are a beggar, be content.

Esaie. [*xxvi.*]
Trust in God, and He will feed you,

and give you what you need:
Dan. xi [*v.*]
as He did Daniel in the lions' den,

And when Elias fled away

[iii. Reg.]
.17.
and Elijah when
ravens fed him.
From Ahab and quene Iesabel,
The rauens fed him by the way,
As the story of Kinges doeth tel.   32

And as King Dauid doth record,

[Psal.] .147.
The rauens byrdes left in the nest,
Are, when they cry, fed of the Lord,
Though they know not to make request.   36

Trust thou therfore in God aboue,

[Psal.] .32.
He will move
men to be
benevolent.
And cal on him with confidence,
And doubtles he will mens hertes moue
To fede the of beneuolence.   40

[Luk] .xii.
[Psal.] .iii.
If you are in
want, do not
despair.
But if at any tyme thou lacke
Thynges nedeful, yet do not despayre,
As thoughe the Lorde did the forsake,
Or ded to the displeasure beare.   44

But in such case, cal to thy mynd
What plenty God hath to the sent,

[Io]b. xiii
You will find you
have wasted
many things,
And thou shalt wel perceiue & find
That thou hast many thynges mispent.   48

Then thincke Gods iustyce coulde not leaue
The unplaged, for that thou hast

[Sa]pt. xi
Mispente the gyftes thou didst receyue
To lyue vpon, and not to wast.   52

Then must thou nedes giue God glorie

[Lu]ke .xv.
for which you
must be sorry.
For his vpryght and iust iudgement,
And be most earnestly sory,
For that thou hast his giftes mispent.   56

But if thou finde thy conscience cleare,
As few men can I am righte sure,
Then let Iobs trouble be thi chere,

Luk [xxi.]
That thou mayst pacientlie endure.   60

Mat [iv.]
Yea though thou shouldest perishe for fode,

Psal [xci.]
Though you
perish, bear it
patiently.
Yet beare thou thy crosse pacientlie ;
For the ende shal turne the to good,
Though thou lye in the stretes & die.   64

Pore Lazarus died at the gate
Of the ryche man (as Luke doth tell) ;
But afterwarde in rest he sate,
When the riche glutton was in hel.   68

Stay thou thi selfe therfore vpon
These examples comfortable,
And doubtles thy vocation
Thou shalt not thinke miserable.   72

Neither shalt thou grudge, or repyne,
That thy pouertie is so greate ;
But shalt thy selfe euer encline
To Goddes wyl, who doth the viset.   76

Thou shalt not grudge when *thou* shalte craue
Of anie man his charitie,
Though at his hand *thou* canst nought haue,
But shalt praie for him herteli,   80

That, if he haue this worldes riches,
And yet hath not Godly pitie,
The spirite of God will him possesse,
And teache him to know his duetie.[1]   84

Thus doing, thou dost walke upright
In thy calling, thou maiest be sure,
And art more precious in Goddes syght
Then men that be ryche paste measure.   88

Thus leaue I the in thi callinge,
Exhorting the ther in to stande ;
And doutles at thy last endyng
Thou shalt be crowned at Gods han[de]   92

Luk. [*xvi.*]
Remembei
Lazarus and the
rich glutton,

Mat. [*xvi.*]
and take comfort
from them.

You must not
grudge or repine,

but pray even
for those who
refuse to give you
when you ask.
i. Joh. [*iii.*]

Mat.x[*xviii.*]
Luke [*iii.*]
Rom. [*ii.*]
Actu. i[*v.*]

Remain in
your calling,
ii. Tim. [*iii.*]
and at last you
will be rewarded.
[*Sapti.*] *iii.*

¶ The Seruauntes Lesson.

Brother, come hither unto m[e]
  And learne some parte of di[s]cipline ;
For I am sent to enstruct th[e,]
And teach the some godlie doctryne.   96

I am sent to
instruct you,
servants, and
give you godly
doctrine.

[1] Orig. ouetie.

I am sent to cal the, I say,
Backe from thy stout & stubborne mynd :
Take hede therfore, and beare away
Such lessons as thou shalt here find.   100

[*Lu*]*k .xvii.*
Your calling is to
work and obey.
    Fyrst, consider that thy callyng
Is to do seruice, and obey
All thy maisters lawful biddynge ;
Bearyng that he shal on the laye.   104

If your master is
cruel, pray to the
Lord,
    If he be cruel unto the,
And ouercharge the with labour,
Cal to the Lord, and thou shalt be
Shortly out of his cruel power.   108

[*Ex*]*odi .i.*
and remember
the Israelites in
Egypt,
    Remember thou Iacobs kynred,
That in Egypt were sore oppreste ;
But when they were most harde bested,
The Lorde brought them to quiete reste.   112

    They could not cry so sone, but he
whom God heard. Had heard and graunted their requeste :
And right so wil he do by thee,
And se al thi great wronges redreste.   116

[*M*]*at. xxv*
he will deliver
you out of
bondage,
    He wyl, I say, deliuer the
Out of bondage and seruitude,
And bringe to passe that thou shalt be
Maister of a great multitude.   120

    And bicause thou didest walke vpright,
Shewyng thy selfe obedyent,
and make your
servants obey
you. Thy seruauntes shall haue styl in sighte
The feare of God omnipotent.   124

    And like seruice as thou hast done,
Thou shalt haue done to the againe :
Mat. [*vi.*]
and, [*vii.*] For sence the world was first begonne,
Neuer true seruaunt lost his payne.   128

Jacob served 14
years, and
Gen. [*xxix*]
became rich,
    Iacob serued full fourtene yere,
And dealt truly with his maister,
As in the Bible doth appeare,
And was exceadinge rich after.   132

Fourtene yere he serued Laban,
Who was made riche be hys laboure;
But afterward, Iacob began
To growe to much greater honour.   136   and increased in honour.
    Laban was neuer of such might   Laban was neuer so mighty as Jacob.
As Iacob was within short space:
For his true seruice, in Gods sight,
Had purchest him fauour and grace.   140
    Thus seest thou how God doth regard
The good seruice of seruauntes trne,
And how he doth in them rewarde
The seruice that is but their due.   144
    It forceth not what maner man   i Petr. [ii.]   It does not matter what your master is.
Thy maister is, so that thou be
In thy seruice a Christian,
Doynge as Christ commaundeth the.   148
    But if thy maister be wicked,   If he wishes you to do wrong, you must have faith,
And would haue the do wickedlie,
Then se that thy fayth be pitched
On thy Lord God most constantly.   152
    Call to thy mynde good Daniel,   and call to mind Daniel's conduct.
Who serued his prince fayethfully,
Notwythstandynge he was cruel,
And eke his Lorde Gods enemy.   156
    Serue him trulye, I say, for why
God hath bade that thou shouldest do so;
But do thou nothinge wickedly,
Neyther for wel nor yet for wo.   160
    Se thou serue him as faythfully   Serve your master faithfully, as if he were your God,
As he were thy Lord and thy God;
Not wyth eye-seruice fainedly,
Neithyr for the feare of the rodde;   164   [Eph]es .vi.
    But for the conscience thou dost beare
To thy Lorde Gods commaundemente;   [Col]oss .iii.
That is, for loue, and not for feare   but only for love, not fear.
Of any worldly punyshmente.   168

7

Do thus, and then thou shalte be sure
Thy Lord wil euer prospere the ;
And at his good wil and pleasure,
Thou shalt not mysse to be made fre.   172

If you are sturdy you will be punished,

But if thou wilt be styl sturdy,
And do thy seruice wyth grudgyng ;
The Lord shall plage the worthely,
With manifulde kindes of scourginge.   176

and put to drudgery,

Thou shalt be put to drudgery
Many a daye, maugrea thyne head ;

and kept in slavery.

And be kepte stil in slauery
Al thy life dayes, til thou be deade.   180

If you run away, you will be caught, or get a worse master.

And if thou chaunce to renne awaye,
Either thou shalt be brought agayne,
Or else, when thou doest chaunce to staye,
A worsse master shal the retayne.   184

Once thou shalt be certeine of this,

If you refuse your calling, you are sure to come to a bad end.

That, if thou refuse thy callyng,
Of misery thou shalt not mysse,
Though thou escape sodaine fallynge.   188

Yea though thou do prosper a whyle,
And seme to haue fortune thi frende,
Yet thou dost but thy selfe begyle,
For miserye shal be thine ende.   192

As you have done, so shall men do to you.

For as thou didest thy maister serue,
So shall al thy seruauntes serue the ;
And as thou didest his goodes preserue,
So shall thy goodes preserued be.   196

Besides, God punishes the disobedient,

And beside thys, Gods wrath is bent
Toward the for disobedience ;
Wherfore, onles thou do repent,
He wyl adde thereto vehemence.   200

and He will punish you wondrously.

He wyl plage the here wonderously,
And at the end cast the in paine,
Wher thou shalt lye eternallye,
And wysh to be a slaue agayne.[1]   204

              [1] Orig. rgayne.

Repent therfore, I the aduise,
And seke thine owne saluation ;
And then thou must in any wise
Walke stil in thy vocation.　　　　　　　　208

　　Do thy seruice dilygently,[1]　　　　　Repent, and do
And shew no disobedience ;　　　　　　your duty
Be thou not stoute, but stil apply　　　reverently.
And do all thynges with reuerence.　　212

　　Refuse nothing that must be done,　　Refuse nothing
But do it wyth al redines ;　　　　　　that must be
And when thou hast it once begon,　　　done :
Then set asyde all slouthfulnes.　　　216

　　Be true, trusty, and tryfle not ;　　be true, trusty,
Be gentle and obedient ;　　　　　　　and don't trifle.
And blessyng shal lyght on thy lot,
For doyng Gods commaundement.　　　220

　　To make an ende : haue stil in minde
Thyne estate and condition,　　　　　　Remember your
And let thyne herte be styll enclynde　condition, and
To walke in thy vocation.　　　　　　　keep in it.
　　　　　　　　　　　　　　　　　224

The Yeomans Lesson.

Thou that arte borne *the* ground to tyll,　　You that are a
　　Or for to laboure wyth thyne hande,　　tiller of the
If thou wilt do nought *that* is yil,　　　ground, must not
Desyre not idle for to stande.　　　　　228　remain idle,

　　But se thou do plowe, plant, and sow,　　you must plow,
And do thy nedeful busines,　　　　　　plant, and sow.
As one that doth his duty knowe,
And wyll not the Lords wyll transgresse.　232

　　For what doste thou, if thou desyr　　If you desire to
To be a lord or gentleman,　　　　　　be a gentleman,
Other then heape on the Gods ire　　　you will gain
And shewe thy se[l]fe no Christian ?　236　God's anger.

　　　　　　[1] Orig. diligenthy.

[*J*]*ohn .x.*   For Christes shepe do hear hys voyce,

[*E*]*xodi .xx.*   Whych biddith the worke busily

                Sixe days, and in the seuenth reioyce,

                And geue somewhat to the nedy.   240

Beware of the desire to be higher,   It doth also byd the be ware

                Of the desyre to be alofte :

                For he that doth for honour care

                Falleth in Sathans snares ful oft.   244

                 Haue minde, therfore, thyselfe to holde

and keep within your degree.   Within the bondes of thy degre,

                And then thou mayest euer be bold

                That God thy Lorde wyll prosper the.   248

If you have plenty, don't be greedy, *Psal.* 62   And though the Lord geue the plentye

                Of corne, cattell, and other thynge,

                Be thou neuer the more gredy,

Prou. 24   Nor set thy mynd on gatheringe.   252

                 But thinke the Lorde doth these thynges sende

                To the, as to his stuard true,

but give where there is need.   That wilt not his goodes wast & spende,

                But bestow them wher they be due.   256

If you get rich, don't set your mind on clothes and dainty food,   And if wyth thy labour thou get

                Money much more then thou doste nede,

                Do not thy mynde on rayment set,

                Neither on deynty fode to fede.   260

                 Set not (I say) thy minde on pride,

                Neither upon delicious fare,

but remember the poor, and be contented.   Neither forget at any tyde

                To geue the pore that thou mayest spare.   264

                 But when thou hast sufficient

                Of fode and honest apparrayle,

                Then holde thy selfe therwyth contente,

i. Tim. v[*i.*]   As wyth the wage of thy trauayle.   268

If you have anything left, give it as God commands you.   The reste (if ought remayne vnspent

                Upon thyne owne necessity)

                Bestowe as he that hath it sent,

                Hath in hys word commaunded the.   272

And yf thou fyfid not written there
That *thou* mast heape thy chest wyth golde,
To bye greate liuelode for thyne hyere,
Howe darest thou then be so bold   276

   Howe darest thou be bolde, I say,
To heape up so much goulde in store,
Out of the due that thou shouldest paye
To them that be pore, sicke, and sore ?   280

   Wo be to them, sayth Esaie,
That heape togither house and lande ;
As men that woulde neuer fynde stay,
Tyll all the earth were in theyr hande.   284

   What, wil ye dwel alone (sayeth he)
Upon the earth that is so wyde ?
Wyll you leaue no parte therof free
From your unsatiable pryde ?   288

   Ye nede not to be so gredy,
For the Lorde doth you playnly tell,
That greate houses shall stand empty,
And no man lefte therin to dwell.   292

   And Moses sayth that *th*ou shalt builde
Houses, and neuer dwell therin
Thyself, nor leaue them to thy chyld,
Nor any other of thy kynne.   296

   And why ? bicause thou hast no mynd
To kepe the Lords commaundement,
But sekest euer for to fynde
Wayes to encrease thine yerely rent.   300

   No maner threatnyng can the let
From purchasyng the deuill and all ;
It is all fysh that commeth to net,
To maintaine thy great pryde wyth all.   304

   Well, turne agayne I the aduise,
And learne to walke in thyne estate,
And set Gods feare bifore thyne eies,
Lest, when thou wouldst, it be to late   308

    CROWLEY.   5

Side-notes:

How dare you hoard up riches!

Esaie .v.
Isaiah pronounces a woe upon all such.

Your great houses shall stand empty.

[*D*]*eu xxvi*[*ii.*]
You shall never dwell in them,

because you have no mind to keep God's commandments.

All is fish that comes to your net—you would buy the Devil.

But repent, and
walk in your
vocation.

i. Cor. [vii.]

And haue in thy mynde euer more,

Thys rule of thy profession,

Whych is in dede Gods holy lore,

To walke in thy vocation.   312

If you should not
prosper, still
thank God.

But if the Lorde do the not blesse

In thy labours wyth greate plenty,

Yet thanke thou hym neuer the lesse ;

Thou hast more then thou arte worthy.   316

If your rent is
raised, pray for
your landlord.

If thy landelordè do reise thy rent,

Se thou paye it wyth quietenes ;

And praye to God omnipotent,

To tak from hym his cruelnes.   320

So shall you
obtain a blessing.

So shall *thou* heape coles on his heade,

And purchase to thy selfe greate reste :

By the same man thou shalt be fedde

By whom thou wast bifore oppreste.   324

For God, who ruleth ech mans herte,

Shal turne thy landlords hert, I saye,

And shall all his whole lyfe conuert,

So that he shall by thy greate staye.   328

If he is not
worthy to repent,
God will destroy
him,

Or else, if he be not worthy

To be called to repentaunce,

No doubt thy Lorde wyll hym distroy,

Or take from hym his heritaunce.   332

and you will be
set free.

Sure thou shalt be he wyll the set[1]

Free from thy landlords tyranny ;

For he dyd neuer yet forget

Any that walked orderly.   336

If you take the
remedy into your
own hand,

But if thou wylt neds take in hande

Thyne owne wrong for to remedy,

The Lord hym self wyll the wythstande,

And make thy lan[d]lord more gredy.   340

it will be all the
worse for you.

And wher before *thou* paidst great rent,

Thou shalt now lose thy house and all ;

Bicause thou couldest not be contente

With patience on him to cal.   344

[1] Orig. looks like see.

In like sort, if thy prince wil take
More tribute then thou canst well spare,
See thou paye it him for Goddes sake,
Whose officers al princes are. 348

For in his nede both thou and thine
Are his to maintaine his estate ;
It is not for the to define
What great charges thy king is at. 352

Yea, though thou se euidently
That he wasteth much more then nede,
Yet pay thy duty willyngly,
And doubtles God shal be thy mede. 356

Now touching thy religion :
If thy prince do commaunde the ought,
Against Goddes Euangelion,
Then praye for him styl in thy thought. 360

Pray for him styl, I say, that he
May haue Godly vnderstanding
To teach Gods word to such as be
Committed to his gouerning. 364

And se thou do not him dispyse,
But aunswere him wyth reuerence ;
And though *thou* mightest, yet in no wyse
Do thou forget obedience. 368

¶ Take not his swerde out of his hande,
But lay thy necke downe under it,
Yea, thoughe *thou* mightest his force withstand ;
For so to do for the is fit. 372

Thy maister Christ hath taught *the* wel
When he would no resistence make :
Neither agaynst the powers rebell,
When men were sent him for to take. 376

Yet if the Lord haue geuen to the
Such knowledge, that thou art certaine
Of thy fayth, knowyng it to be
Of the truth, do therin remaine. 380

Side notes:

Pay all your, taxes, *Mat .xii.*

and remember it isn't for you to say what the king shall spend.

Even if you see his waste, it is your duty to pay.

If the king commands you to act contrary to the gospel,

you must still pray for him,

and answer him with reverence.

a. xiiii. You must not take the sword into your own hand.

Math 26.

If you are certain of your faith, remain in it.

Math .x.

For though man may thy body kyl,
Yet oughtest thou not him to feare ;
For he can do thy soule none yll :
Wherfore be bold, do not dispaire.   384

Be bold to
confess Christ—
He can save you
from all ill,

Be bold, I say, Christ to confesse
Wythout feare of this worldly paine ;
For when thou shalt be in distresse,
Christ shal acknowledge the agayne.   388

Luke .xxi
and will
acknowledge you,
if you conquer.

Christ shal acknowledge the, I say,
If thou conquire by sufferyng ;
And do thy selfe hereupon stay,
That thou must walcke in thy callynge.   392

But if you lift
your hand
Ma. xxvi
against the king,

But if thou do lyfte up thy sword
Agaynst thy kynge and soueraine,
Then art thou iudged by Gods word
As worthi therwith to be slayne.   396

or repine against
him,

Yea, thou maist not grudge or repine
Against thy kynge in any wise,
Though thou shouldst se plaine *with* thine eien
That he were wicked past al sise.   400

Pro .viii.
remember he is
appointed by
God, and,

For it is God that appointeth
Kinges and rulers ouer the route :
And with his power he anointeth
Them for to be obeyede, no doubte.   404

if he is evil, to
punish your sins.

If they be euil, then thinke thy sinne
Deseruith that plage at Gods hande;
And se thou do forthwyth bigynne
Thyne owne wickednes to wythstande.   408

Korah and
Dathan rebelled,

Corah and Dathan dyd rebell,
And thought *that* thei them selues culd poynt
A better prieste in Israell
Then Aaron, whom God dyd annoynte.   412

But what came of their phantasie ?
Was not distruction theyr ende ?

and were
destroyed.

God dyd distroye them sodenly,
Bicause thei woulde his workes emende.   416

Let this example suffice the,

To kepe the in obedience

To such as God shal set to be

Ouer the in preheminence.　　　420

　　If thou do thus, thou shalt be sure

That God thy Lord wyll euer so

That, though thy rulars be not pure,

Yet they shall euer defende the.　　424

　　Contrariwise, if thou rebell,

Be sure the Lorde wyll the distroye ;

Which thyng hath ben declared wel

Wythin this realme very lately.　　428

　　For notwythstanding *that* oure kynge,

And eke oure rulers euerychone,

Be mercifull in theyr doynge,

Yet haue the rebelles cause to mone.　　432

　　And why ? bicause no rebelles shall

Escape Gods hand vnpunished ;

For God hym selfe doth princis call

Hys Christes and hys annoynted.　　436

　　Whoso therfore doth them resiste,

The [s]ame resisteth God certayne ;

For God hym selfe doeth them assiste

Agaynst them ouer whom they raygne.　　440

　　If thou therfore fynde the greeued

Wyth men set in Autoritie,

Seke thou not to be auenged,

But let God take vengeaunce for the.　　444

　　Let me take vengeance, saith the Lord,

And I wyll quyte them all theyr hyre :

Do thus, and scripture doth recorde

That thou shalt haue all thy desyre.　　448

　　Thou shalt haue thy desyre, I saye,

Upon the wicked maiestrate,

If thou wylt kepe thy selfe alway

Wythin the boundes of thine estate.　　452

Let their fate keep you in obedience,

and then your rulers will defend you.

If you rebel, as you did lately, you will be destroyed.

Princes are God's anointed,

and those who resist them resist Him

Rom xi[ii.]

to whom vengeance *Eccle.* [xii.] belongs.

Rom. x[ii.] Keep yourself within bounds, and you will have your desire of wicked magistrates.

You'll go to hell
if you will
change.

Thus leaue I the, wyth threatenyng
To the thy soulles damnation,
If thou, mislykynge thy callynge,
Wylt nedes change thy vocation.   456

The Lewde or Vnlerned Priestes Lesson.

Listen, Sir John,
and I will say
something to
you.

Thou that art lewde wythoute learnynge,
  Whom communly men cal syr Iohn,
Geue eare, for I wyll saye somethynge
Concernyng thy vocation.   460

You are ignorant,
and without good
qualities.

Thou art a man voide of knowledge,
And eke of all good qualities,
Only mete for to dych and hedge,
Or else to plant and graffe mens trees.   464

You are not an
offerer of
sacrifice,

Thou art not, as thou woldst be calde,
An offerer of sacrifice;
For though thy crowne were iiii tymes bald,
Yet canst thou not so bler our eies.   468
  For it is plaine in holy wryte,

for none can offer
for sin,
[H]ebru .x.

That none can offer sacrifices
For sinne, either in flesh or sprite,
Though he be boeth learned and wyse;   472

since Christ was
offered for all,
[H]ebru. ix

For Christe was once offered for all,
To satisfie for all our synne,
And hath made fre that erste were thral,
The faythful flocke of Iacobs kynne.   476
  To offer sacrifice therfor,
Thou arte not called, I tell the playne;

[R]om .xi.

For Christe lieueth for euermore,

and He can no
more be slain.

And can no more for vs be slayn.   480
  Thy state therfore, and thy callyng,
Is none other than for to wyrcke,

[Thr]enc. .iii.

And not to liue by forestallyng,

[Pr]ov .x.

And name thy selfe one of the kyrcke.   484

If thou therfore wylt lyue for aye,
And reigne with Christe for euermore,
Desyre no mo masses to saye,
But get thy fode wyth laboure sore. 488

If you desire to
live for ever,
don't seek
masses.
[*E*]*phe .iiii.*

Geue over all thy tippillyng,
Thy tauerne gate, and table playe,
Thy cardes, thy dyce, and wyne bibyng,
And learne to walke a sobre waye. 492

Give over tippling
and gambling.
[*E*]*phes .v.*

And if thou haue any lyueyng,
So that thou nede not to laboure ;
Se thou apply the to learnynge
Wyth all thy busy endeuonre. 496

i Tim i[*v.*]
and apply
yourself to
learning,

But to thys ende se thou study,
That, when thou hast the truth learned,
Thou maist profite other thereby,
Whom in tyme paste thou hast harmed. 500

that you may
profit others.

And se thou go not idelly
From house to house, to seke a place
To saye men a masse secr[e]tly,
Theyr fauoure thereby to purc[h]ase. 504

Do not say
masses in secret,
leading men to
think popish
customs will be
restored,

Put not the ignorant in hope
That they shall se all vp againe,
That hath ben broughte in by the Pope,
And all the preachars put to payne. 508

But if thou canste do any good
In teachyng of an A B C,
A primar, or else Robynhode,
Let that be good pastyme for the. 512

If you can do
good by teaching
A B C, do so.

Be euer doyng what thou can,
Teachyng or learnyng some good thyng ;
And then, lyke a good Christian,
Thou doste walke forth in thy callynge. 516

Always do as
much good as you
can.

But if thou wylt knowledge reiect,
And all honeste laboures refuse,
Then arte thou none of Gods elect,
But art wo[r]sse then the cursed Iewes. 520

If you reject
labour and
knowledge. you
are worse than a
Jew.
Rom. .c.

¶ Repent therfore, I the aduise,
And take wholsome councell bityme ;
And take good hede in any wise,
That knowledge double not thy crime.　　　524

I will pray that
you may leave
your popishness. Thus leaue I the, makynge promes
To make for the petition,
That thou mayst leue thy popyshnes,
And walke in thy vocacion.　　　528

The Scholars Lesson.

Come hither, young man, vnto me ;
　　Thou that arte brought up in learnynge,
Give ear, young
man, Geue eare awhile ; I wil teach the
How thou shalt walke in thy callynge.　　　532

and observe that
schools were
founded First mark wherfore scholes were erecte,
And what the founders did intende ;
And then do thy study directe,
For to attaine vnto that ende.　　　536

　　Doubtles this was al their meaning,
for such learning
as the country
had need of. To haue their countrei furnyshed
Wyth all poyntes of honest learnynge,
Whereof the publyke weale had nede.　　　540

　　Call thou therfore to memorie
What knowledg thy contrei doth lacke,
And apply the same earnestly,
By all the meanes that thou canste make.　　　544

When you have
decided what
knowledge to get,
get it at once, And when thou art determined
What knowledg thou wilt most apply,
Then let it not be loytered,
But seke to get it spedily.　　　548

and do not idle. Spende not thy tyme in idlenes,
Nor in vayne occupation ;
But do thy selfe wholly addres
To walke in thy vocation.　　　552

Se thou do not thy mynde so set
On any kynde of exercise,
That it be either stay or let
To thy studye in ani wise :   556

To fyshe, to foule, to hunt, to haulke,
Or on an instrument to play ;
And some whyles to commune and talke,
No man is able to gayne saye.   560

For field sports
and music no
man can blame
you.

To shote, to bowle, or caste the barre,
To play tenise, or tosse the ball,
Or to rene base, like men of war,
Shal hurt thy study nought at al.   564

Archery, casting
the bar, tennis,
and such games,

For all these thinges do recreate
The minde, if thou canst holde *the* mean ;
But if thou be affectionate,
Then dost thou lose thy studye cleane.   568

serve for
recreation, if
used moderately.

And at the last thou shalt be founde
To occupye a place only
As do in Agime ziphres rounde,
And to hynder learnyng greatlye.   572

For if thou hadst not the lyueing,
Another shoulde, that wold apply
Him selfe to some kynde of learnynge,
To profyte his contrey therby.   576

If you did not
occupy your
living another
would, who might
do better.

If thou therfore wilte not be founde
Worthy Goddes indignacion,
Make thy studye perfecte and sounde,
And walke in thy vocacion.   580

Make your study
perfect.

Let not tyme passe the idelly,
Lose not the fruite of any houre ;
Or else suffer hym to supply
Thy place, that wyll hym endeuoure.   584

Do not be idle;

Thou doest but rob *the* commone wealth
Of one that would be a treasur ;
Better thou were to lyue by stelth,
Then for to worke such displeasure.   588

if you are, you
only rob the
commonwealth.

There is no need
for you to resign
your living,

¶ But haply thou wylt say agayne,

Shall I surrender my lyuyng ?

Shall I not therupon remayne,

After I haue gotten learnyng ?   592

    ¶ Yesse thou maiste kepe thy lyuyng still,

Tyll thou be called other wise ;

but you must
keep yourself
[L]uke .xix.
exercised,

But if thou wylt regarde Gods wyll,

Thou must thyself styll exercise.   596

    When thou art thorowely learned,

and must teach
others,
[L]uke .xix.

Then se thou teach other thy skyll,

If thou wylt not be reconed

For a seruant wycked and ill.   600

    ¶ Teach them, I saye, that thou dost se

Wyllynge to learne thy discipline,

and let your life
be as a book
before them.

And vnto them se thy lyfe be

A boke to laye before theyre eine.   604

    Let them neuer se the idle,

Nor heare the talke vndiscretely ;

And by all the meanes possible,

Rom. 14.

Let all thy doynges edifie.   608

    Thus leaue I the, wyshynge that thou

Maiste, by thys admonition,

Henseforth desyre, as I do nowe,

To walke in thy vocation.   612

The Learned Mans Lesson.

Don't you learned
men disdain to
learn of me.

Thou learned man, do not disdayne,

    To learne at me, a symple wyght,

Thy greate abuses to refrayne,

And in thy callyng to go ryght.   616

    Thou arte a man that sittest hye

In the simple mans conscience ;

If you live
dissolutely, you
are an offence to
the simple.

To lyue therfore dissolutly,

Thou shouldste be vnto them offence.   620

¶ Offence, I say, for thou shoulde think
All that thou doste to be godly ;
Wherfore do not at this thynge wynck,
But do emende it spedily.

Emende thy wycked lyfe, I say,
And be (in dede) a perfecte lyght,
As Christe our Savioure dothe say,
And let thy workes shine in mens syght,
  For it is thy vocation
To leade other the redy waye ;
Howe greate abominotion,
Arte thou then if thou go astraye ?

But herein lyeth the whole matter,—
To know which waye thou shouldest then lead :
Wherfore I wil not the flatter,
But tell the truth wythouten dreade.

Thou must thy selfe humiliate,
And acknowledge thy wycked sinne,
And stryue to enter the streyt gate,
Where fewe men do fynde a waye in.

¶ This way thou canst not walke, so longe
As thou wylt trauaile sea and lande,
And frame all the wordes of thy tonge,
To get promotion at mans hande.

Thou must humble thy selfe I saye,
And not aye seke to be alofte ;
For he that walketh in rough waye,
And loketh hye, stombleth ful oft.

Thou must acknoledge that thou arte,
Through synne, vnworthy thyne estate,
And that thy discipline and arte
Can not brynge the in at that gate.

Thou must, I saye, stryue to enter,
And not to get promocion ;
Thy lyfe thou must put in venture
For Christes congregation.

624 *Math* [xviii.]
Amend your life and serve as a light to others.

628

i. *Corh* [iv.]
If you lead men astray, you are an abomination.

632

636

You must humble yourself, and acknowledge your sin. *Mat.* [vii.]

640

You cannot do this while you are seeking promotion from man.

644

648

You must confess your unworthiness.

652

John. x

You must venture your life for Christ.

656

How dost thou walke in thys callyng,
When thy mynde is earnestly bent
To gather up eche mans falling,
By al the wayes thou canst inuent?   660

Mat .vii.
Give ear, you fool,
and learn your
first lesson again,

Geue eare, I saye, therefore thou fole,
And learne thy fyrst lesson agayne :
Enter into Gods holi schole,
And do not hys doctryne dysdayne.   664

He wylleth the fyrst to apply
Thy mynde to knowledge, and to take

[L]uke .vi.
and take the
beam out of your
own eye,

The great beame out of thyne own eye,
And thine abuses to forsake.   668

And then he wolde, that in no wyse
Thou shouldest be slacke or negligente

then you will
pick the motes
from other men's
eyes.

To pycke the motes out of mens eyes,
Teaching them how they should repent.   672

If thou wylt that thei do repente,

[T]ite .ii.

Repent thou fyrst, that they maye see
That the whole some of thyne intente
Is to make them like vnto the.   676

If you wish
others to repent
and forsake their
sins,

For, if thou wylt them to refraine
Mur[t]her, thefte, whoredome, & inceste,
If they se these thynges in the raigne,
They wyl al thy doctryne deteste.   680

If thou forbid them gluttononye,
And wil them the flesh for to tame,

you must set
them an example.

They wil defie the vtterly,
If they se the not do the same.   684

If you speak of
their apparel,
you must be
faultless yourself.

If thou tel them of apparayle.
Or of ought wherin is excesse,
Then wil they say, thou doest but rayle,
Vnlesse thou be therin faultles.   688

If you speak of
usury or simony,
see that you are
free.

What shouldest thou speake of vsurie,
When thou dost take vnlawfull gayne?
Or rebuke men for Simonie,
When nothynge else doeth in the rayne?   692

Maye not the lay man saufly saye,
I learned of the to by and sel
Benefices ? whych, to thys daye,
Thou canst put in practise ful well.

696

Why should not a
layman have two
or three benefices
as well as you?

Why should not I, as well as thou,
Haue benifices two or thre ?
Sens thou hast taught me the wei how
I may kepe them and blamelesse be.

700

He can set others
to serve the cure
as learned as you
are;

I can set one to serue the cure,
That shall excel the in learninge,
More then thou dost me, I am sure ;
And also in godly lyueynge.

704

he can give as
much to the poor
as you give.

I can kepe hospitalitye,
And geue as much vnto the pore
In one yere, as thou dost in thre,
And wyl performe it wyth the more.

708

Alas! that
Christ's flock
should be so
bought and sold.

Alas ! that euer we should se
The flocke of Christ thus bought & solde,
Of them that shoulde the shepherdes be,
To leade them saifly to the folde.

712

¶ Repent this thyng, I the aduise,
And take the to one cure alone ;
And se that in most faythfull wise,
Thou walk in thy vocation.

716

Take to one cure
and be faithful,

Then shall no lay man saye, by right,
That he learned his misse of the ;
For it is playne, in ech mans syght,
That thou dost walke in thy degree.

720

then none can
blame you.

Morouer, if thou chance to be
Made a prelate of hygh estate,
To thyne office loke that thou se,
And leaue not thy flocke desolate.

724

If you are a
prelate, look to
your office;

And fyrste, before all other thynges,
Seke thou to fynde good ministers,
And appoynt them honest lyuynges,
To be the peoples instructers.

728 [i] *Tim .v.*

seek for good
ministers;

8

have none in
whom is any
vice.
Let none haue cure wythin thy see,

In whome any greate vice doth reigne ;

For where mislyuyng curates be,

[*Ez*]*ech* .33.
The people are not good certayne.   732

If any perish
through you, you
will have to
answer for them.
[*i*] *Tim. v.*
And for them all that do perishe

Through thy defalte, thou shalt answere ;

Wherefore, I do the admonishe

To loke earnestly to thys geare.   736

Loke vnto it thy selfe, I saye,

Do not trust to
any trifler,
And truste not to a tryfelar,

That wyll allowe all that wyl paye

Somewhat vnto the regester.   740

and see that the
young are
instructed.
Se that they do instruct the youthe

Of eche paryshe diligently,

And trayne them vp in the Lords truth,

So much as in theyr powre shall ly.   744

If you are called
to be the prince's
counsellor,
Now if so be thou be called,

To be thy Princes councelloure,

Beware thou be not corrupted

By the vayne desyre of honoure.   748

Be not carful how for to holde

Thy selfe styll in autoritie ;

be bold to speak
the truth,
But to speake truth be euer bolde,

Accordyng to Goods veritie.   752

¶ Winke not at faltes that thou shalt se,

Though it be in thy Souerayne ;

But do as it becometh the :

and exhort him
to leave his sins,
Exhort hym all vice to refrayne.   756

If thou perceyue him ignoraunt

In any parte of hys dutie,

Se thou do hym not checke or taunte,

But tell hym wyth sobrietie.   760

and tell him his
faults with all
submission.
Tell hym his falte, I say, playnly,

And yet wyth all submission ;

Lesse thou do seme to speake vaynly,

Forgettyng thy vocation.   764

Thus haue I tolde the, as I woulde
Be tolde, if I were in thy place ;
To the intent that no man shoulde
Haue cause to tel the to thy face.   768

   Thus do I leaue the wyth wyshyng
To the a wyll for to aduaunce
Gods glorie by godly learnyng,
And not thy lyuyng to enhaunce.   772

*Thus I have told
you your duty.*

The Phisicians Lesson.

Geue eare, maister Phisicion,
  And set asyde thyne vrinall,
And that wyth expedition,
For I the laste trumpet do call.   776

   Geue eare, I say, and mark me well ;
And printe all my wordes in thy mynde,
For ech thyng that I shall the tell
Thou shalt boeth true and certen fynde.   780

   God made the to succour mans nede,
As Iesus Sirach wryteth playne,
But by due proufe we know in dede
That many thousandes thou hast slaine.   784

   But now am I sent from the kynge
Of powre and domination,
To call the from thy murtherynge,
To walke in thy vocation.   788

   First, wher thou didest heretofore vse
To haue respect to the ryche man,
I woulde not now thou shouldest refuse
To helpe the pore man if thou can.   792

   Helpe hym, I saye, though he be pore,
And haue nothynge wherwith to paye,
For hys maister hath yet in store
A crowne for him at the laste daye.   796

*Attend, Master
Physician, and
mark my words
well.*

*God made you to
succour man,
[Ec]cles. 38*

but you kill him.

*You have paid
respect to the
rich; now help
the poor,*

*even when he has
nothing with
which to pay.*

796 [*T*]*ob .ii.*

Cure him for
God's sake, and
He will reward
you.

And if thou do on him thy cure,
For hys sake *that* geue herbes their stre*n*gth,
Thou shalt vndoubtedly be sure
He wyll rewarde the at the length.   800

Thys maister of hys doth regarde
[*Ma*]*th. ix.* Mercie so much, that he hath tolde
He rewards those All hys that they shal haue rewarde
who give a cup
of water. For geuynge water thyne and colde.   804

And thinckest thou that he wyll not
Rewarde them that geue medicine ?
Thou hast no such mistruste, I wot,
In hys promise that is diuine.   808

If you can cure
the poor, you
may be sure of
your reward.

I saye therfore, if thou canst cure
The pore mans sore or maladi,
Of thy rewarde thou shalt be sure,
If thou wylt shewe on hym mercie.   812

If you neglect
him because he
has no gold, your
trust shall fail.

But if thou suffer hym to lacke
Thyne helpe, bicause he lacketh goulde,
No doubt when thou shalt acompt make
Thy confidence shall be full colde.   816

What authority
have you for
neglecting the
poor ?

Then shew thy writynge if thou can,
Wheron thou bearest the so bolde,
That thou wylt viset no sicke man
That cannot lyne thy pursse with golde.   820

Brynge forth thy writyng the*n*, I say,
If thou haue any such in store,
Wherby thou maiste require eche daye
A noble of golde or else more.   824

What right have
you to charge for
looking at water,

And shewe by what right thou maist take
Two pe*n*ce for the sight of water,
When thou knowest not therbi to make
The sicke man one farthinge better.   828

Yea, if a man should try the wel,
To proue what thy counnyng can do,
when you cannot He should fynde that thou canst not tell
tell whether a
man is ill or not ? Whether the man be sycke or no.   832

¶ I graunt the water sheweth somthyng,
But not so much as thou dost crake ;
Neither is thy laboure condynge
That thou shouldest money for it take.   836

Water may show something, but not much.

But if so be thou canste espy
By the water what is amisse,
Teach hym how to seke remedy,
And worthy some rewarde that is.   840

But if thou do but gesse, as doeth
The blyndeman that doth cast hys staff ;
Though thou by chaunce hit on the soth,
Thy labour is scase worthy chaffe.   844

If you only guess, but chance to hit the truth, your labour is not worth much.

Thou dost but gesse money to wyn,
And wyth strang words make men agast ;
And yet thou thinckeste it no synne
To cause pore men theyr goods to wast.   848

You only guess to win money.

But now, I saye to the, repent,
And do thy selfe henseforth applye
To vse the gifte God hath the sent,
To the profite of thy contrey.   852

Repent, and apply yourself to profit your country.

Let not lucre make the professe
Before thy knowleege be perfect ;
For he that ministreth by gesse,
Shall not so sone heale as infect.   856

Apply the earnestli therfore
To get phisikes perfection ;
That thou maiste ease the sike and sore,
And remedy infection.   860

Strive to ease the sick and remedy infection.

And shut not vp thine helpe from suche
As stande in moste nede of the same ;
And certes thou shalt gaine as much
By them, as by men of greate fame :   864

Help the poor and needy, and

For God hymselfe hath promised
To make for them a recompence
Wherfore doubt not to be paied,
Both for thy laboure and expence.   868

[M]ath .16.
[L]uk .10.
God will recompense you.

CROWLEY.   6
E *

But if thou wylt not take my rede,
But folowe after lucre styll,
I wyll put the out of all dreade
Thy last rewarde shall be full ill.   872
For when cruel death shall the styng,
And thy lyfe from the separate,
Then shalt thou se thou hast nothyng,
Thy silly soule to recrate.   876
Wherfore I must nedes greatly feare
That in that extreme agonie,
Thou wylt of Gods mercie dispare,
And so perishe eternally.   880
Take hede therfor, take hede by time,
Let not slyppe this occasion ;
But spedily repent thy cryme,
And walke in thy vocation.   884

Side notes:
If you will not listen,
when you die
you will despair of God's mercy.
Take heed while you have time.

The Lawiars Lesson.

Nowe come hither thou manne of lawe,
    And marcke what I shall to the saye,
For I intende the for to drawe
Out of thy moste vngodly waye.   888
Thy callyng is good and godly,
If thou wouldste walke therin aryght ;
But thou art so passing gredy,
That Gods feare is out of thy syght.   892
Thou climist so to be alofte,
That thy desyre can haue no staye ;
Thou hast forgotten to go soft,
Thou art so hasty on thy way.   896
But now I call the to repent,
And thy gredines to forsake,
For Gods wrath is agaynst the bent,
If thou wylt not my warnyng take.   900

Side notes:
Your calling, the Law, is good if you walk aright, but you are so greedy,
there is no limit to your desires.
God's wrath is bent against you.

Fyrst call vnto thy memorye
For what cause the laws wer fyrst made ;
And then apply the busily
To the same ende to vse thy trade.   904

Remember why laws were first made.

The lawes were made, vndoubtedly
That al suche men as are oppreste,
Myght in the same fynde remedy,
And leade their lyues in quiet reste.   908

They were made to relieve the oppressed.

Doest thou then walke in thy callyng,
When, for to vexe the innocent,
Thou wilt stand at a barre ballyng
Wyth al the craft thou canst inuente ?   912

I saye ballyng, for better name
To haue it can not be worthye ;
When lyke a beast, withoute al shame,
Thou wilt do wrong to get money.   916

Is it well for you to stand bawling like a beast to get money ?

Thyne excuses are knowne to well,
Thou saist thou knowest not the matter,
Wherfore thou sayst thou canst not tel
At the firste whose cause is better.   920

You say you don't know whose matter is right ;

Thou knowest not at *the* first, I graunt,
But whye wylt thou be retained
Of playntyfe, or of defendaunt,
Before thou hast their cause learned ?   924

but why are you retained before you learn the cause ?

For such a plea I blame the not,
When neither parties right is knowne ;
But when thou thy selfe dost well wot
Thy client seketh not his owne,   928

I do not blame you for this plea, when neither party's right is known.

It were a godly way for the
To knowe the ende ere thou began,
But if that can bi no meanes be,
To make shorte sute do what thou can.   932

If thou be a mans atturney,
In any court where so it be,
Let him not waite and spende money,
If his dispatch do lie in the.   936

If you are attorney for any man, don't delay his case,

Apply his matter earnestly,
And set him going home againe,

and take no more
than your due.
Luke x[iv.]
And take no more then thy dutie ;
For God shall recompence thi paine.   940

If you are a
counsellor, don't
be a trifler ;
If thou be calde a counseller,
And many men do seke thy read ;
Se thou be found no triffeller,
Eyther for money or for dreade.   944

But weigh mens matters thorowlie,
And se what may be done by right,

assist the poor as
well as the rich :
Leuit. [xix.]
And further as well the neadie
As thou woldest do the man of might.   948

respect no man's
person.
Se thou haue no respect at all
To the person, but to the cause ;
And suffer not suche truth to fall
As thou findest grounded on good lawes.   952

If a wrong-doer
wishes you to
defend him,
don't.
If any man do the desyre
Him to defend in doinge wronge,
Though he woulde geue the triple hire,
Yet geue none eare unto his songe.   956

Fear no man's
power, but fear
the Lord.
Fear not his power, though he be king,
A duke, an earle, a lord, or knight ;
But euermor in thy doinge
Haue the Lordes feare present in syght.   960

If you are a
judge, beware of
bribes,
If thou be iudge in commune place,
In the kinges bench, or Exchequier,

[*i*] *Parl.* 22.
Or other courte, let not thy face
Be once turned to the briber.   964

lest they blind
your sight.
Beware *that* bribes blinde not thy sight
And make the that thou canst not se
To judge the pore mans cause aryght,

Deut .xvi.
When it is made open to the.   968

Eccles .xx.
Admit no delays.
Why shouldest thou stil admyt delaies
In matters that be manifest ?
Why doest thou not seke all the wayes
That may be to rid the oppreste ?   972

To thine office it doeth belonge
To iudge as iustice doth require ;
Though the party that is to stronge,
Would geue the house and land to hire. 976

I haue no more to say to the,
But warne the that thou be contente
To lyue only vpon thy fee,
Fearyng the Lorde omnipotente. 980

And for to see that no man wrest
The lawes, to do any man wronge ;
And that no pore man be oppreste,
Nor haue his sute deferred longe. 984

Now if thou be Lord Chauncelloure,
As censor ouer al the rest ;
Se thou do thy best endeuour
To see al open wronges redrest. 988

And of this one thynge take good hede,
That amonge them that do appeale,
Thou do not, for fauoure or mede,
Suffer any falsely to deale. 992

Beware of them, I saye, that vse
First for to tempt the commune lawes,
And yet the iudgement to refuse
When they be like to lose their cause. 996

Beware of them, and let them not
Abuse thy courte in any wyse,
To werie suche as, by iuste lotte,
To cleim their ryght do enterpryse. 1000

When they shall make peticion
Examine them diligently,
And graunt not an iniunction
To eche false harlot by and by. 1004

Graunt thou not an iniunction
To him that doth nought else entende,
But, by subtile inuention,
His owne falsehode for to defend. 1008

Leuit. xix
and do justice to
all men.

I warn you to be
content with
your fees,

and to see that
the poor are not
oppressed.

If you are Lord
Chancellor, see
all wrongs
redressed,

and show no
favour.

Beware of such
as refuse to abide
by the laws.

Be careful in
granting
injunctions.

I nede not to tel any more
Of thy duetie ; thou maiest it se
In Gods sacred and holye worde,[1]
If thou wylt there to applie the.   1012

    Thus leaue I the, thou man of lawe,
   Wyshing the to be as wyllyng
To folowe, as I am to draw
The backe agayne to thy callynge.   1016

The Marchauntes Lesson.

Nowe marke my wordes thou marchaunte man,
    Thow *that* dost vse to bie and sell,
I wyll enstruct the, if I can,
How thou maiste vse thy callynge well.   1020

    Fyrst se thou cal to memori
The ende wherfore al men are made,
And then endeuour busily
To the same ende to vse thy trade.   1024

    The ende why all men be create,
As men of wisdome do agre,

Is to maintaine the publike state
In the contrei where thei shal be.   1028

¶ Apply thy trade therfore, I sai,
To profit thy countrey with al ;
And let conscience be thy stay,
That to pollinge thou do not fal.   1032

If thou venter into straunge landes,
And bringe home thynges profitable ;
Let pore men haue them at thine handes
Upon a price reasonable.   1036

Though *thou* maist thi money forbeare,
Til other mens store be quite spent,

Yet if thou do so, that thy ware
May beare high price, *thou* shalt be shente.   1040

[1] Orig. lorde.

Thou shalt be shent of him, I say,
That on the seas did prospere the,
And was thy guide in al the way
That thou wentest in great ieopardye.   1044

For he gaue the not thy rychesse,   *God gaue you riches*
To hurt thi contrei men withal;
Neither gaue he the good successe,
That thou sholdst therby make men thral.   1048

But thy richesse was genen to the,
That thou mightest make prouision,   *that you might make necessaries for your country,*
In farre controys, for thinges that be
Nedefull for thine owne nacion.   1052

And when, by Gods helpe, *thou* hast brought   *and when you have brought any good thing home,*
Home to thy coast ani good thing
Then shouldest *thou* thank hym that all wrought
For thy prosperouse returnyng.   1056

Whych thyng thou canst not do in dede,
Unles thou walke in thy callyng;
And for hys sake that was thy spede,   *you should thank Him for your prosperity.*
Content thy selfe wyth a lyuynge.   1060

But oh! me thynke I wryte in vayne   *But I write in vain.*
To marchaunte men of thys our tyme;
For they wyll take no maner payne,
But only vpon hope to clyme.   1064

So sone as they haue oughte to spare,   *Merchants, as soon as they have gained anything, purchase lands.*
Besyde theyr stocke that muste remayne,
To purchase landes is al theyr care
And al the study of theyr brayne.   1068

Ther can be none vnthrifty heyre,   *They smell out unthrifty heirs;*
Whome they will not smel out anon,
And handle him w*ith* wordes ful fayre,
Tel al his landes is from him gone.   1072

The fermes, the woodes, and pasture grou*n*ds,   *they have farms round London;*
That do lye rou*n*d about Lo*n*don,
Are hedged in within their mowndes,
Or else shalbe ere they haue done.   1076

They haue thier spies vpon eche syde

To se when ought is lyke to fal ;

And as sone as ought can be spied,

They are ready at the fyrst cal.   1080

I can not tel what it doeth meane,

But white meate beareth a greate pryce

Which some men thinke is by the meane

That fermes be found such marchaundise.   1084

For what is it when the pore man,

That erst was wont to pay but lite,

Must now nedes learne (do what he can)

To playe eyther double or quite.   1088

If ye aske of the coliar,

Why he selleth hys coles so dere,

And rightso of the wodmongar,

They say marchauntes haue all in fere.   1092

The wood, say thei, *that* we haue bought

In tymes paste for a crowne of golde,

We cannot haue, if it be ought,

Under ten shyllynges ready told.   1096

I am ashamed for to tell

Halfe the abuse that all men se,

In such men as do by and sell,

They be so bad in eche degre.   1100

I wyl therfore do what I can

To make plaine desiaratyon,

How thou, that art al marchauntman,

Maist walke in thy vocation.   1104

Applye thy trade, as I haue tolde,

To the profyt of thy contrey,

And then thou maiste[1] eer be bolde

That thy Lord God wil guide thy wai.   1108

Thou shalt not nede to purchase landes,

Neyther to take leases in groundes,

That, when thou hast them in thyne handes,

Thou maist for shyllinges gather poundes.   1112

· Orig. maisse.

Marginal notes:

they have their spies on every side.

Some think the buying and selling of farms cause white meat to be so dear.

The poor man must now pay double rent, or quit.
The collier and woodmonger

say their prices are doubled.

I am ashamed of the abuses among merchants,

so I will do what I can to teach you your vocation.

Trade for the profit of your country,

then you will not need to take leases of grounds.

Thou shalt not ned? to bie or sel
Benefices, which should be fre,
To true preachers of Gods gospell,
To helpe them with that helpeles be.   1116

    You may neither buy and sell benefices,

No more shalte thou nede for to lende
Thy goodes out for vnlawful gayne,
In such sort that, by the yeares ende,
Thou maist of one shillyng make twaine.   1120 *Luke.* ει

    nor lend for unlawful gain.

    Thou shalt aye haue inough in store
For the and thine in thy degre ;
And what shouldst thou desire more,
Or of hygher estate to be?   1124

    If you have enough, why desire more

    Let it suffice the to mary
Thy daughter to one of thy trade :
Why shouldest thou make hir a lady,
Or bye for her a noble warde?   1128

    Marry your daughter to your equal,

    And let thy sonnes, euery chone,
Be bounde prentise yeres nine or ten,
To learne some art to lyue vpon :
For why should they be gentlemen ?   1132

    and bind your sons apprentice.

    There be already men inowe
That beare the name of gentil bloud ;
Tell thou me then, what nede haste thou
So vainly to bestow thy good?   1136

    There are plenty of gentlemen.

    For thou canst not promote thy sonne,
But thou must bye him land and rent,
Wherby some must neades be vndone,
To bryng to passe thy fonde entent.   1140

    If you promote your son, you must buy him land.

    Some man, perchaunce, nede doeth compel
To morgage hys lande for money ;
And wilt thou cause hym for to sell
The liuelode of his progeny?   1144

    If a man must mortgage his land—why do you compel him to sell ?

    Tel me if *thou* wouldest haue thy sonne
(If haply he should stand in nede)
To be so serued, when thou art gone,
Of marchauntes that shall the succede?   1148

    Would you like your son so served ?

Do thou as thou wouldest be done by,
As very nature doth the teache,
And let thy loue and charitie
Unto all the Lordes creatures reach ; 1152
And if any man stande in nede,
Lende hym frely that thou maiste spare,
And doubtlesse God wyll be thy mede,
And recompence the in thy ware. 1156

Be iuste, playne, and not disceytefull,
And shewe mercie vnto the pore,
And God, that is moste mercifull,
Shall euermore encrease thy store. 1160
And in the ende, when nature shall
Ende thy peregrination,
Thou shalt haue ioye emonge them all
That walkt in theyr vocation. 1164

But, if thou do refuse to walke
In thy callyng, as I haue tolde,
Thy wisdome shalbe but vaine talke,
Though thou be both auncient and olde. 1168
Saye what thou wylt for to defende
Thy walkynge inordinately,
Thou shalt be certen, in the ende,
To be damned eternally. 1172
For in the worlde ther can not be
More greate abhomination,
To thy Lorde God, then is in the,
Forsakeyng thy vocation. 1176

Marginal notes:
[M]at. vii.
Do as you would be done by,

[L]uke. vi. and lend to the needy.

Be just, open, and merciful, [M]ath. v. and God will increase your store.

But if you refuse to do as I have told you,

you certainly will be damned in the Mat. vii. end.

¶ The Gentlemans Lesson.

Thou that arte borne to lande and rent.
And arte cleped a gentleman,
Geue eare to me, for myne intent
Is to do the good if I can. 1180

Marginal note:
You that are born gentlemen,

Thou arte a man that God hath set
To rule the route in thy countrey ;
Wherfore thou hadste nede forto get
Good knowledge rather then money. 1184

For ignoraunce shall not excuse,
When all men shall geue a rekenyng ;
And the iudge wyll money refuse,
And iudge after eche mans doyng. 1188

Fyrst I aduertise the therfore,
And require the in Christes name,
That of knowledge thou get the store,
And frame thy lyueyng to the same. 1192

Get the knowledge, I saye, and then
Thou shalt perceyue thyne owne degre
To be such that, emong all men,
Thou haste moste nede learned to be. 1196

Thou shalt perceyue *thou* haste no tyme
To spare, and spende in bankettyng,
For though thou watch tyll it be pryme,
Thou shalt haue inough to doyng. 1200

Thou shalt not fynde any leasure,
To dice, to carde, or to reuell,
If thou do once take a pleasure,
In vseyng thyne owne callyng well. 1204

For parkes of dere *thou* shalt not care
Neither for costuouse buildyng,
For apparell, or for fyne fare,
Or any other worldly thinge. 1208

Thy mynd shal be styll rauished
With the desyre to walke vpryghte,
And to se al vice punished,
So much as shal ly in thy myght. 1212

Thou shalt delite for to defende
The pore man that is innocent,
And cause the wicked to amend,
And the oppressour to repent. 1216

are set to rule your country-men.

You must get knowledge,
Eccl r[ii.]

for ignorance can be no excuse.
Rom. [xiv.]

Mat. iv.

Get knowledge, and live up to it.

You will see you have no time to spare in feasting.

You will have no leisure for gambling.

hunting, costly building, or apparel.

You must strive to walk upright;

and delight in defending the poor,

and in doing
your duty.

Thou shalt haue delite in nothyng
Sauinge in doynge thy duty;
Which is, vnder God and thy kyng,
To rule them that thou doest dwel by.   1220

You are not
allowed to do as
[*Ro*]*m*. 14.
you like with
your own.

Thou shalt not think *that* thou maist take
Thy rente to spend it at thy wyll,
As one that should no recknyng make
For ought that he doth well or yl.   1224

But thou shalt fynd *that* thou art bound,
And shalt answer much more strayghtly,

[*Lu*]*ke .xii.*

Then the pore men that tyl the ground,
If thou regard not thy duty.   1228

You may not
raise your rents
at will—

Thou shalt not fynd that thou maiest reise
Thy rent, or leauy a great fine
More then hath bene vsed alwayes;
For that only is called thyne.   1232

For as thou doest hold of thy kyng,

you must allow
your tenants to
live.

So doth thy tenaunt holde of the,
And is allowed a lyueinge
As wel as thou, in his degre.   1236

If thou, therfore, wouldest not thi king
Should take of the more then his due,
Why wilt thou abate the liuynge
Of thy tenaunt and cause him rue?   1240

Knowledge will
tell you to do as
you would be
done by,
Mat. vi

For knowledge wyl tel the, that thou
Must do as thou wouldest be done by;
And ryght so wyl she tel the how
Thou maiste discharge al thy duty.   1244

and to be content
with your
inheritance.

She wyl teach the to be contente
Wyth that thou haste by herytage;
And eke to lyue after thy rente,
And not to fal into outrage.   1248

If you can afford
to spend 40*l.*, you
may not live up
to 60*l.*

If thou maye despend xl. pound,
Thou maiste not lyue after three score;
Neyther maist thou enclose thy ground,
That thou mayst make it yerely more.   1252

For knowledge wil teach the to seke
Other mens wealth more then thine owne,
And rather to fede on a leke
Then one house·should be ouerthrowen. 1256

Thou shalt by her learne that *thou* art
A father ouer thy country,
And that thou oughtest to play the parte
Of a father both nyght and day. 1260

Thou shalt by knowledg vnderstand
That thou must succour the neady,
And in theyr cause such men wythstande
As shew themselues ouer gredy. 1264

In fine, knowledge that is godly
Wyll teach the al that thou shalt do
Bilongyng to thyne owne duty,
And other mens duty also. 1268

Gette the knowledg, I saye, therfore,
That thou mayste be worthy thy name ;
For wythout hir thou maiste nomore
Be called a ge[n]tleman for shame. 1272

For wythout knowledg thou shalt be
Of all other moste out of frame ;
Bicuuse there is nothyng in the,
That may thy luste chastice or tame. 1276

Wythout knowledg *thou* wylt folowe
Thy fleshe and fleshly appetyte,
And in the luste therof wallowe,
Settyng therin thy whole delyte. 1280

Wythout knowledge *thou* wylt oppresse
All men that shalbe in thy powre ;
And when they shalbe in distres,
Thou wylt them cruelly deuoure. 1284

Wythout knowledg thou wilt aray
Both the and thyne paste thy degree,
And eke mayntayne outragiouse playe,
Tyl thou haue spent both lande and fee. 1288

You must learn that you are a father to your country,

Psalm 8. and understand that you must aid the needy.

In short, knowledge will teach you your duty—

without it you can't be called a gentleman,

because you have nothing within you to subdue your passions.

Without knowledge you will oppress all men who are in your power,

and dress and gamble till you have spent all.

9

If you have no knowledge you will be worse than a slave.

To make an ende ; vnlesse thou haue
Knowledg remaynyng in thy breste,
Thou shalt be worse then a vile slaue
That doth all honestie deteste.   1292

Study always to know your duty, and to fear God.

Get the knowledg, therfore, I saye
And eke the feare of God aboue ;
And let thy study be alwaye
To knowe what thyng doth the bihoue. 1296

  But fyrste, bifore all other thynges,

[P]salm .33

Set the Lords feare bifore thy face,
To guyde the in all thy doynges,
That thou delyte not in trespace.   1300

He who delights in sin will never get knowledge,

For he that doth delyte in synne
Shall neuer gouerne hys lyfe wel,
Nor any godly knowledge wynne ;
For wisdoume wyl not with him dwel. 1304

so seek her till you find her.
Sapie [vi]

Then seke for knowledg busilie,
And leaue not off tyll she be founde ;
And when thou hast her perfectelie
To the Lordes feare let her be bounde. 1308

  And let them two beare all the swea
In thy doinges, earelye and late[1] ;

Let the fear of God and knowledge

Let them agre and ende their plea,
Before thou do appoint the state.   1312

  By theyr aduise suruei thy lande,

guide you in all things,

And kepe thy courtes both farre & nere,
And se they do fast by the stande,
In thine housekeping and thy chere. 1316

and have them ever in mind.

Haue them present before thine eies,
In al thy dedes what so they be ;
In cessions, and eke on assise,
Let them not be absent from the.   1320

Let them rule your family,

Let them rule all thy familie,
And eke enstruct thy childrene yonge ;
That they may thyne office supply
When with hys darte death hath the stong. 1324

     [1] Orig. lare.

And last of all, leaue them to guyde
Thy chyldren and theyr families;
That thy house and floke may abyde,
And rule the route in godly wise.   1328

   and your
   children's
   children.

    No more to the I haue to saye
But that thou kepe Gods feare in syght
And make it the guyde of thy waye
As well by bryght daye as by nyght.   1332

    So doyng I dare the assure
That in the ende thou shalt obteyne
The blisse that shall euer endure,
Wyth Christe our Maister for to rayne.   1336

   So doing you
   shall obtain the
   bliss of heaven.

¶ The Maicstrates Lesson.

Whoso thou be that God doeth call,
    To beare the swerd of punishment,
Mark wel my words and take them all
Accordyngly as they be ment.   1340

   You who are
   called magis-
   trates

    When thou arte in autoritie,
And haste the bridle rayne in hande;
Then be well ware that tirannie
Do not get the wythin hir bande.   1344

   and have the
   bridle-rein in
   hand,

    Loke not vpon thy swerd alway,
But loke sometyme on thy ballaunce,
And se that neither do decay
In the tyme of thy gouernaunce.   1348

   look at the
   balance as well
   as at the sword,

    For to punyshe wyth equitie,
Is, and aye shalbe, bisemeyng;
Whereas to shewe extremiti,
Is founde rather a bloude suckeyng.   1352

   and punish with
   equity.

    If any man be accusede
Se thou hear him indifferently,
And let him not be punished,
Tyl thou knowe his cause thorowly.   1356

   Be impartial in
   your judgment,

If he haue wrought against *the* lawes,
So that iustice woulde haue him dye,
Then in thy ballaunce laye his cause,
And iudge him after equitie.   1360

If a man err
through ignor-
ance or poverty,
If he dyd it of ignoraunce,
Of nede, or by compulsion,
Or else by fortune, and by chaunce,
Then must thou vse discretion.   1364

consider what
extreme need is,
Consyder what extreme nede is,
And howe force may the weake compel,
And how fortune doth hit and misse,
When the intent was to do well.   1368

and that wit-
nesses may lie.
And though the euidence be plaine,
And the accusars credible ;
Yet call to mynde the elders twayne,

Dani [*xiii.*]
That Daniell found reproueable.   1372

    ¶ And if thou fynde them false, or vayne,
Forged to worcke theyr brother yll,
Then let them suffer the same paine
That he shoulde haue had by their wyll.   1376

I might say
much under this
head,
Much myght be sayde in this matter
Out of the workes of writers olde,
And, for to proue it the better,
Many late stories might be tolde.   1380

but I leave it to
your study.
But I leaue this to the study
Of them that haue had exercise
In iudgement, in whose memorie
It is as styll before theyr eyes.   1384

I thought mete to tuch it only,
That thou myghtest haue occasion
Your duty is
To call to mynde the chief dutie
Of thy state and vocation: 1388

to weigh
evidence, and
examine accusers,
Whych is to scanne the euidence,
And eke to try the accusars all,
Thoughe they be men of good credence,
Leste happly the iuste be made thral.   1392

More ouer it behoueth the,
I[f] thou wylt walke in thy callyng,
To se that all good statutes be
Executed before al thynge.   1396   and to see the
                                                            statutes enforced,

For to what ende do statutes serue,
Or why should we hold parliamente,
If men shall not suche lawes obserue
As in that court we shal inuent?   1400

And what thynge shall a realme decay   because neglect
So sone, as when men do neglecte   of statutes makes
The wholsom lawes, as who should sai,   a realm decay,
They were in dede to none effecte.   1404

For in that realme the mightie shal
Worke after theyr fancie and wyl;
For there the pore may crie, and cal   and brings
For helpe, and be oppressed styl.   1408 oppression upon
                                                         the poor.

Se thou therfore to thy dutie
In this behalfe, both daie and night,
And let none break such lawes freli,
But let them know *that* lawes haue might.   1412

Let them al know, I say, that thou   Let men know
Art set to minister iustice,   you are set to
And that thou madest therto a vowe   administer
At the takeing of thine office.   1416 justice.

Wincke not at thynges *that* be to plaine,   Do not wink at
Lest godly knowledge fle the fro,   things which are
And thou flyt into endeles payne,   too plain.
At such time as thou must hence go.   1420

For if thou wilt not minister   If you will not
Iustice to them that do oppresse,   administer
What are the people the better   justice,
For the when they be in distresse?   1424

The heauenly housband man, therfore,
Who planted the, vice to suppresse,
Shall drye thy rote for euermore,
And geue the vp to wyckednes.   1428
        CROWLEY.   7

9 ★

Jhon. xv
beware of the
vengeunce of
God ;

Beware of thys vengeaunce betyme,
Lest it come on the sodaynly,
When *thou* wouldest faine repent thy cryme,
But shalt despeire of Goddes mercy.   1432

For what thing causeth men despeire
Of Gods mercy at their last ende,

your conscience
will make you
despair.

But their conscience, that saieth thei were
Told of their fault, & woulde not mende ?   1436

If thou therefore doest se this thynge,
And wylt wincke at it willinglye,
I say that, when death shal the styng,
Thou shalt despeire of Gods mercye.   1440

I have more to
say yet.

Yet haue I more to say to the
Concernyng thy vocation,
Which, if it grow styl, must nedes be
Double abhomination.   1444

For he that bieth must nedes sel :
Thou knowest alreadye what I meane ;
I nede not wyth playne wordes to tel,
If sinne haue not blinded the cleane.   1448

See that you
allow no offices
to be sold.

Se vnto it, I the aduise,
And let not offices be solde ;
For God wyll punyshe in straite wyse
Such as wyth him wyl be so bolde.   1452

God will not
permit His flock
to be devoured
of wolves.

He wyl not aye suffer his flocke
Of wolfes to be so deuoured,
Neither shall they *that* would hym mocke,
Escape his handes vnpunyshed.   1456

His arme is as stronge as it was

Remember
Pharaoh
Exo. xiiii.

When he plaged Kyng Pharao
In Egipt, and can bring to passe
Al that he listeth now also.   1460

He spent not al his power vpon

[*Dan.*] *iiii.*
and Nebuchad-
nezzar,

The Kyng Nabuchodanozer ;
He shal neuer be found such one,
That he should not haue mighte in store.   1464

Take hede, take hede, I saye therfore,
That thou fal not into his hand ;
For if thou do, thou art forlore,
Thou canst not þe able to stand.

and take heed
that you fall not
[*Hebru*]e .*.*.
into His hand.

1468

Yet one thynge more I must the tell,
Which in no wyse thou mayst forget,
If thou wylt professe Gods Gospel,
And thyne affiaunce therin set :

If you profess
the Gospel,

1472

Thou must not couet imperye,
Nor seke to rule straunge nacions ;
For it is charge inough, perdie,
To aunswere for thyne owne commons.

you must not
seek power.

1476

Let thy study, therefore I saye,
Be to rule thyne owne subiectes wel,
And not to maynetayne warres alwaye,
And make thy contrey lyke an hell.

Study to rule
your own
subjects well.

1480

Let it suffice the, to defende
Thy limites from inuasion ;
And therein se thou do intende
Thine owne peoples saluation.

Defend your own
country from
invasion,

1484

For, marke this : If thou do invade,
And get by force commodite,
The same shal certenly be made
A scorge to thy posteritye.

and do not invade
other lands.

1488

This haue I sayde, to call the backe
From the Philistines stacion ;
Trustynge thou wylte my counsell take,
And walke in thy vocacion.

[*i*] *Reg. xiii.*

1492

The Womans Lesson.

Whoso thou be of woman kinde,
 That lokest for saluation,
Se *thou* haue euer in thy mynde,
To walke in thy vocacion.

All women should
walk in their
vocation.

1496

If you have no
husband, improve
your manners.

If thy state be virginitie,

And hast none housband for to please,

Then se thou do thyselfe apply

i. Cor. vii. In Christen maners to encrease.   1500

If thou be vnder a mestres,

If you have a
mistress, serve
her readily.

Se thou learne hir good qualityes,

And serue hyr wyth al redines,

Haueyng Goddes feare before thine eies.   1504

If thou se hir wanton and wilde,

Then se thou cal vpon God styl,

That he wyl kepe the vndefilde,

And kepe from the al maners yl.   1508

Avoid idle talk
and nice looks.

Auoyde idle and wanton talke,

Auoyde nyce lokes and daliaunce;

And when thou doest in the stretes walk,

Se thou shewe no lyght countenaunce.   1512

Dress according
to your condition.

Let thyne apparayle be honest;

Be not decked past thy degre; ·

Neither let thou thyne hede be dreste

i. Timo. ii. Otherwyse then besemeth the.   1516

Neither dye your
hair,

Let thyne haare beare the same coloure

That nature gaue it to endure;

Laye it not out as doeth an whore,

That would mens fantacies allure.   1520

nor paint your
face,

Paynte not thy face in any wise,

But make thy maners for to shyne,

And thou shalt please all such mens eies,

As do to godlines enclyne..   1524

but be modest,
learn your
duties,

Be thou modeste, sober, and wise,

And learne the poyntes of houswyfry;

And men shall haue the in such price

That thou shalt not nede a dowry.   1528

and try to please
God.

Studye to please the Lorde aboue,

Walkynge in thy callyng vpryght,

And God wil some good mans hert moue

To set on the his whole delite.   1532

Nowe when thou arte become a wyfe,
And hast an housbande to thy mynde,
Se thou prouoke him not to stryfe,
Lest haply he do proue vnkynde.

Acknowledge that he is thyne heade,
And hath of the the gouernaunce ;
And that thou must of him be led,
Accordyng to Goddes ordinaunce.

Do al thy busines quietly,
And delyte not idle to stand ;
But do thy selfe euer applye,
To haue some honest worcke in hand.

And in no case thou maist suffer
Thy seruauntes or children to play ;
For ther is nought that may soner
Make them desire to renne awaye.

Se thou kepe them styl occupyed
From morne tyl it be nyght agayne.
And if thou se they growe in pryde,
Then laye hand on the brydle rayne.

But be thou not to them bytter,
Wyth wordes lackyng discretion,
For thine housband it is fitter
To geue them due correction.

But if thou be of such degre
That it is not for the semely
Emonge thy maydens for to be,
Yet do thy selfe styl occupye ;

Do thy selfe occupy, I say,
In readinge, or hearyng some thynge,
Or talkyng of the godly way,
Wherein is great edifiyng.

Se thy children well nurtered,
Se them brought vp in the Lordes feare,
And if their meaners be wycked,
In no case do thou wyth them beare.

If you have a
husband,

1536 [i C]or .xi.

let him guide
you.

1540

Be industrious.

1544

and keep your
children and
servants from
idleness.

1548

1552

But do not be
too severe.

1556

If you are above
mixing with your
servants,

1560

spend your time
in reading.

1564

See that your
children are well
brought up.

1568

If your husband
does wrong,
admonish him
mildly.
And if thine housbande do outrage
In any thinge, what so it be,
Admonish him of hys last age,
Wyth wordes mylde as becommeth the.   1572
And if he do refuse to heare
Thy gentle admonicion,
Yet se if thou can cause him feare
Goddes terrible punission.   1576

Allure him by
your godly
living.
Do what thou canst, him to allure
To seke God by godly liueing,
And certenly thou shalt be sure
Of life that is euerlastinge.   1580

For though the
first woman fell,
For though the first woman did fall,
And was the chiefe occasion
That sinne hath pearsed through vs all,
Yet shalt thou haue saluation.   1584

you shall be
saued if you are
obedient,
Thou shalt be salfe, I say, if thou
Kepe thy selfe in obedience
To thine housband, as thou didest vow,
And shewe to him due reuerence.   1588

and do all in
faith.
But in fayth must all this be done,
Or else it doeth nothynge anayle ;
For without fayeth nought can be wone,
Take thou neuer so greate trauayle.   1592

Thou must beleue, and hope that he,
That bade the be obedyent,
Wyll be ryght well pleased wyth the,
Because thou holdest the content.   1596

But if your
husband is godly,
Nowe, if thyne housbande be godly,
And haue knowleged better then thou,
learn of him,
Then learne of him al thy dutie,
And to his doctryne se thou bowe.   1600

[i Ti]mo. v.
Se thou talke wyth him secretly
and do all that
he approves.
Of su[c]h thinges as do the behoue ;
And se thou obserue thorowlye
[i Ti]mo. c.
Al such thinges as he shal aproue.   1604

Seke to please him in thine araye,
And let not newe trickes delyte the;
For that becometh the alway,
That with his minde doth best agre. 1608

Delite not in vaine tatyllars,
That do vse false rumoures to sowe;
For such as be great babbelars
Wyll in no case their dutie know. 1612

Delight not in
tattlers—

Their commynge is alwaye to tell
Some false lye by some honeste man;
They are worsse then the deuell of hell,
If a man would them throughly scanne. 1616

they are worse
than the devil;

They wyll fynd faute at thyne araye,
And say it is for the to base,
And haply ere they go awaye,
They wyl teach the to paynt thy face. 1620

Yea, if al other talke do fayle
Before the idle tyme be spent,
They wyl teach the how to assayle
Thyne housband with wordes vehemente; 1624

they will teach
you to scold your
husband,

Thow muste swere by Goddes passion,
That long before thou sawest his heade.
Thou hadest ech gallaunt fassion,
And wilt agayne when he is deade. 1628

and tell him of
your tricks
before you knew
him.

Thou must tell him, that he may heare,
Wyth a lowd voyce, & eke wordes plaine,
That *thou* wilt sometyme make good chere
With ryght good felows one or twaine. 1632

I am ashamed for to wryte
The talke that these gossepes do vse;
Wherefore, if thou wylt walke vpryght,
Do theyr companye quite refuse. 1636

I am ashamed of
these gossips,

For they are the deuelles mynysters,
Sent to destroy al honestye,
In such as wyl be their hearars,
And to theyr wycked reade applye. 1640

for they are the
devil's ministers.

i. Pet. iii.
But do you learn
of Sara,

But thou that arte Sarais daughter,
And lokest for saluation,
Se thou learne thy doctryne at hir,
And walke in thy vocation.   1644

Gene. xxvi.
who always
obeyed her
husband.

She was alway obedyent
To hir housband, and cald hym lorde,
As the boke of Godes testament
Doeth in most open wyse record.   1648

Follow her, and
you will be safe
in the end.

Folowe hir, and thou shalt be sure
To haue, as she had in the ende,
The lyfe that shall euer endure :
Unto the whiche the Lorde the send.   1652

Amen.

.

Imprynted at

London bi Robert Crowley
dwellinge in Elie rentes
in Holburn.   The yere
of our Lord .M.
D. xlix. the
laste daye of December.
☞ Autore eodem Roberto Croleo.
¶ Cum priuilegio ad imprimendum solum.

Pleasure

And Payne, Heauen and Hell:

Remembre these foure,

and all shall be

well.

¶ Compyled by Roberte Crow=
ley, Anno Domini, MDLI.

Cum priuilegio ad imprimendum
solum.

¶ O ye that be my fathers blessed ones
come and posses the kyngdome that
was prepared for you befor the
beginning of the worlde.

¶ Goe ye curssed sorte into the euerla-
stynge fyre that was prepared for
the Deuill and his Angelles.

Math. xxb.

¶ To the ryght worshypful Lady   [Page 3]
Dame Elizabeth Fane, wyfe to the
ryght worshypfull Syr Rafe
Fane Knyghte : Roberte
Crowley Wyshethe
the Lyfe euer-
lastynge

AFter I had compiled thys litle treatise (ryght ver-
tuouse Lady) I thought it my duty to dedicate *I thought it my duty to dedicate this treatise to you.*
the same vnto youre Ladishyppes name, as to a ryght
worthy Patrones of al such as laboure in the Lords
harueste. Not for that I thyncke I haue herein done
any thyng worthy so liberall a Patrones, but for the
worthynes of the matter, whych is a parte of the holy
gospel of Iesu Christ wrytten by the holy Euangelyste
Mathewe, and is most necessary to be beaten into the
heades of all men at thys daye, to dryue them (if it be
possible) from the gredy rakeyng togyther of the treasures of this vayne worlde. I do not doubt, but if God
haue not geuen men vp to their owne herts lust, they *If men are not given up to their own hearts' lust, they will begin to live the gospel which they have [Page 4] talked.*
wyll nowe at the laste endenoure to lyue the gospell
which they haue of longe tyme talked. In dede it was
ne*cessarie that God should styr vp some to plage such
emonge his people as had offended euen as he dyd often
tymes styr vp the heathen to plage hys people of
Israell ; but yet it is not necessarye that the same
should continue in oppressyng the offendars and inno-

cent togither.   For so shal they also deserue the Lordis
wrath, & in the ende be plaged by some other that God
shal styr vp to reuenge the iniurye done to the innocent
sorte.   Moued therefore wyth the desyre to se the

God's anger will
fall on the land if
oppression and
covetousness do
not cease.

wealth of my contrey by the pacifiyng of Gods ire,
which (no doubt) wyl fal vpon this realme very shortly,
if oppression and gredye couetise cease not, I haue, so
playnely as I coulde, set forth in thys litle boke the
terrible iudgment of God (which no doubt of it is at
hande), that if there remayne any feare of God in mens
hertis, it may cause them to staye at the least waye, and
not to procede any farder in the inuentyng of newe
wayes to oppresse the pore of thys realme, whoes oppression doeth alredy crye vnto the Lorde for venge-

May the Lord so
work in the
hearts of the rich,
that the venge-
ance fall not in
our days.

ance.   The Lorde work in the hertis of the rych, that
this vengeaunce fall not on thys realme in oure dayes,
for doubtles it wyl be gret when it cometh.   And if

[Page 5]

the oppression cease not, the vengeance can not
ta*rye longe.   For the Lorde hath promised
to reuenge his people in haste.   This
Lord preserue your good Ladiship
to hys good pleasure in thys
lyfe and geue you blysse in
the lyfe to come.
So be it.

    Your   Ladyships   at   commaundement,   Robert
Crowley.

[Page 6, blank]

When Christ shall come to iudge vs all,[1]
  And geue eche one as he hath wrought,
Hys Fathers frendis then wyll he call,
  To enioye that whych they haue sought,
  By beleueng that they were bought
Wyth his bloude shedde vpon a tree,
As by theyre workis all men maye see.

[Page 7]
When Christ
Mat. xvi.
comes to iudg-
ment He will call
His friends to
4 enjoy what they
have been seek-
ing.

7 *Mat. vii.*

"Come! come!" shall he saye to these men,
  "Come, and possesse for euermore
That kyngdome, whych my Father, when
  No worlde was made, layed vp in store
  For you, whome he dyd knowe before
To be in maners lyke to me
That am his Sonne, and aye haue be!

He will bid them
come and possess
Mat. xxv.
the kingdom pre-
pared for them,

11

[Page 8]
Rom. viii.

14

"Come!" shall he saye, "for aye, when I
  Stode nede of meate, ye gaue me fode;
So dyd you drynke when I was drye,
  Reioyceng when you dyd me good.
  No fende, therefore, shall chaynge your mode;
For you shall alwayes be wyth me,
And shall my Fathers godheade se.

because when He
was hungry they
fed Him.

Mat. xxv.

18

They shall re-
main ever with
Him, and see
God.
21 *i. Cor. xiii.*

"And at all tymes, when I haue bene
  Of nedefull lodgeynge desolate,
You haue bene gladde to take me in;
  Whether it were yarly or late,
  You dyd me neuer chyde nor rate;
But gaue me wordis curteyse and kynde,
Procedynge from a faythfull mynde.

Mat. xxv.

When He was
desolate, they
25 [Page 9]
took Him in,

and treated Him
courteously.
28

    [1] Two lines of the original are put into one.

1 0

¶ " So, when I was naked and bare,

When He was
naked, they
Mat. xxv.
clothed Him.

Hauynge no clothes my fleshe to hyde,

From your owne backes then dyd you spare,

And gaue me clothes for backe and syde,   32

So that I myght the colde abyde.

But if you lackt sufficient,

Then dyd you my greate lacke lament.   35

When He was
sick and in
[Page 10]
prison, they com-
forted Him,
and visited Him,
Mat. xxv.
and ransomed
Him.

" Infyne, when I was weake and sycke,

And had no conforte aboute me,

To come to me you dyd not stycke,

And succour my necessitie.   39

And when it chaunced me to be

In prisone, and could not get oute,

To raunsome me you went aboute."   42

Mat. xxv.
The just will ask
when they ever
saw Him in
need?

¶ Then shall the iuste answere agayne

And saye, " O Lorde, when sawe we the

In prisone, or in other payne

Through extreme nede and pouertie ?   46

Is He not Lord of
land and sea?

Arte not thou Lorde of lande and see ?

What? Lorde, we knowe that sea and lande

[Page 11]

Haue euermore bene in thyne hande ;   49

1. *Cor. iiii.*
He gives all
things to all men,
and every man is
in His hand.

" We know that thou gaueste all thynge

To all estates, booth hygh and lowe.

There is no myghty lorde nor kynge,

But he is in thyne hande we knowe.   53

In vayne, Lorde, we might plante and sowe,

If thou gaue vs not frute and grayne,

We coulde haue nought lyfe to sustayne."   56

He owns He gave
us life and fed us,

Then shall Christe saye, " All this is true ;

I gaue you lyfe, and dyd you fede

Wyth graynes and fruitis, booth olde and newe,

And gaue you all thyngis at your nede.   60

[Page 12]
and has been
with us in all our
ways.
John xv.

In all your wayes I was your speede,

And gaue you that wherefore ye sought,

Wych wythout me had come to nought.   63

☞ " Yet all that I haue sayde before
Is true also ; for when you gaue
Ought to such as were sycke or sore,
Whome nede constray[ned] forto craue,   67
Then, I confesse my selfe to haue
Receyued all that at your haude,
Whereof they dyd in greate nede stande."   70

But when we gaue anything to the sick we gaue it to Him.

Mat. xxv.

¶ Then shall the iuste wyth ioye enter
Into the ioyes that shall not ende ;
By cause theyr hertes were aye tender
To geue such thyngis as God dyd sende,   74
Maukynde from peryle to defende.
Thus shall they lyue in ioye and blysse
In Paradice, where no payne is.   77

The just will enter into everlasting joys,

[Page 13] because their hearts were tender. Mat. v.

They will live in Paradise.

But to the wycked Christ shall saye,
" Auoyde frome me, ye wycked sorte ;
For in my nede you sayde me naye
Wyth spytefull wordis of disconforte.   81
Yet my preachars dyd you exhorte
Me in my membres to refreshe,
Knoweynge that all are but one fleshe."   84

To the wicked He will say, " Depart! for in my need ye Mat. xxv. refused me."

1. Corhi. x

☞ Then shall these men, wyth faynte herte, saye
" Lorde when dyd we see the in nede ?
Thou haste bene Lorde and Kynge alwaye ;
No wyght was whome thou dydest not fede :   88
All this we learned in oure Creede ;
For thou arte Iesus, that Gods Sonne
That hath create boeth sonne and mone."   91

[Page 14, Mat. xxv. They will answer, " Lord, when did we see thee in need?

Thou art Jesus, who created all things."

☞ " Oh," shall Christe saye to them agayne,
" Ye deafe dorepostis, coulde ye not heare !
Thynke you the heade bydeth no payne,
When the members make heauye chere ?   95
In you nought but flesh doeth appere.
For if my spirite in you had ben,
Me in myne you must nedis haue sene.   98

He will answer, " You deaf doorposts,

1. Cohr. xii.

[Page 15] if my spirit had been in you, you must have seen the poor.

¶ "The pore, the pore, and indigent
  Came vnto you ofte tymes ye knowe,

You did see
them weep, but
did not help
them.
And you sawe them wepe and lament,
    Yet would ye not on them bestowe   102
    The leaste frute that to you dyd growe.

No, no, you were redy to take
  That other gaue them for my sake.   105

"Your hertis were harder then the flynt—

Ezech. 33.
There was no
pity in your
hearts.
[Page 16]
    In them no pitie coulde be founde.

Your greedye gutte coulde neuer stynt,
    Tyll all the good and fruitfull grounde[1]   109
    Were hedged in whythin your mownde.

How did you
use your lands
and goods?
You wycked sorte, howe vsed ye
  The londis and goodis ye had of me?   112

☞ "You made your boaste all was your owne,
  To spare or spende, at your owne wyll;

When a poor
man called your
Mat. xxi.
acts in question,
you put him into
prison.
And when any pore men were knowne
    That were so bolde to calle it yll,   116
    My landis and goodis in waste to spyll,

You shet them vp in prisone strong,
  Tormentynge them euer emonge.   119

"False libertynes you dyd them call,

[Page 17]
Because a man
told you your
duty, you said he
wished to have
all.
    Because they tolde you your duitie.

You sayde the loselles woulde haue all
    That you had goten paynfully,   123
    And kept longe tyme moste carefully;

But ye belye them, I know well,
  And slaunder this my true Gospell.   126

But mine only
wish for their
own,

as I shall tell
you.
Luke .xvi.

[Sign. with Dr
Bliss MS. note,
"P. B. i. 34
[Page 18]
1 Q 8"]
☞ "Emonge all myne there is not one
  That would haue ought more then his owne,

As I shall tell you playne anone;
    For to me all theyr hertis be knowne.   130

They reaped nought that you had sowne,
But wylled you to let them haue
  That I gaue you mankynde to saue.   133

                    Orig. nownde.

"Not one so blynde emonge you all,
   But he knoweth I made all of nought,   *You know I made all things,*
Appoyntynge all thyngis naturall,
    To serue mankynde, whome I haue wrought   137   *Psal. viii.*
    Lyke to my selfe in loueyng thought ;   *Gensis. i.*
Wyllynge that eche should at his nede,
Haue breade and broth, harbour and wede.   140

"But syth it was expedient   *that the needs of all might be supplied,*
   That emonge all there should be some
Alwaye sycke, sore, and impotent,
    I indued you wyth such wysedome   144
    As dyd honest stuardis become,   [Page 19]
Committyng [1] whole into your hande   *Mat. 24.*
The riches, boeth of sea and lande.   147

"My purpose was that you should haue   *and that you might have a store to succour the needy.*
   Alwaye all nedefull thynges in store,
To succour such as nedis must craue
    Of you thyngis nedefull euermore.   151
    I made you rych to fede the pore ;
But you, lyke seruauntis prodigall,
Haue in excesse consumed all.   154   *Mat. 24.*

"But when I found you negligent   *When I found you negligent*
   In fedynge of my family,
Then my prophetes to you I sent,   [Page 20]
    Commaundyng that you should yerely   158   *I sent my prophets to you,*
    Brynge all your tythes diligently   *Malc. iii.*
Into my barne, that there myght be
Meate in myne house for ponertie.   161

"But you gaue to theyr wordis no hede ;   *but you heeded them not,*
   You helde all faste, and woulde nought brynge
Into my barne the pore to fede,
    But spent all at your owne lykynge   165   *and spent all in wantonness,*
    In wantones and banketynge,   *Gene. 32.*
And in rayment past your degree,   *and raiment.*
As men that had no mynde of me.   168

[1] Cammittyng in original.

CROWLEY.   9

[Page 21]

¶ " Yea, some of you were not content
   To holde fast that ye should haue brought
Into my barne, there to be spent ;

Iohn .x.
You begged
and bought that
which was mine,

   But gredyly ye begde and bought,   172
   That my true seruantis, as they ought,
Dyd at my true prophetis byddynge,
Into my barne faythfully brynge.   175

and, when once
in my fold,

¶ " And when you had once goten in,
   Into my folde, emonge my shepe,
Then you thought it to be no synne
   Styll in your kennells forto slepe,   179

set others to keep
my flock.
[Page 22]

   Settyng such ones my flocke to kepe,
As were more lyke to eate the lambe,

Iohn .x.

Then to defende his feble dame.   182

Ezech. 34.
You spoiled my
flock and me.

☞ " Ye robde, ye spoylde, ye bought, ye solde
   My flocke and me ; in euery place
Ye made my bloude vylar then golde :
   And yet ye thought it no tre[s]passe.   186
   O wycked sorte, voyde of all grace,
Auoyde from me downe into hell,
Wyth Lucifer : there shall ye dwell.   189

You had the
tithes,
Ezech. 34.

" Ye had the tythes of mens encrease,
   That shoulde haue fedde my flocke and me ;
But you made your selfes well at ease,

[Page 23]

   And toke no thought for pouertie.   193

and were not
sorry to see my
flock and me
have need.

   It dyd not greue you forto se
My flocke and me suffer greate nede
For lacke of meate, harbour and wede.   196

¶ " No hell can be a worthy payne
   For your offence, it is so greate ;
For you haue robbed me, and slayne
   My flocke for lacke of nedefull meate.   200
   The woule, the lambe, the malt, and wheate,

You carried
all away.

You dyd by force cary awaye,
And noman durst once saye you naye.   203

¶ " Howe can you loke to haue mercie
   At myne hande ? whome ye would not feede   [Page 24]
Wyth that was myne, euen of dutie   What mercy can
   To succoure me and myne at nede ?   207   you expect ?
   Syth you myght in the scripture rede,
That suche men shall no mercie haue
As kepe theyr owne when nede doethe craue.   210 *Iacob. ii.*

" Unto the hungry parte thy breade,   *Esai.* [*l*]*viii*
   And when thou shalt the naked se,
Put clothes on him ; this myght you reade   You might have
   In my prophetis that preached me.   214   seen in the Scriptures
   And in Iohns Pistle these wordis be :—
' Howe can that man haue Charitie,
That beynge riche sheweth no pitie ? '   217   [Page 25]

" Also, the man that stoppeth his eare   *Prou. xxi.*
   At the crye of such as be pore,   that he who would not hear the poor
Shall crye, and no man shall him heare,
   Nor at his nede shewe him succoure :   221
   Ryght so he that doeth endeuoure   *Prou. xxii.*
To be made rych by oppressynge,
Shall leaue him selfe (at the last) no thynge.   224   should not be heard.

" For he shall geue the ryche alwaye
   More then he can scrape frome the pore,
So that in tyme he shall decaye,
   And haue no nedefull thynge in store.   228
   This might you reade, and ten tymes more   [Page 26]
In the Bible, that holy boke,   if you had had time to read.
If you had had tyme forto loke.   231   *Math. x.*

" But such scriptures you coulde not broke
   As bade you geue ought to the pore ;
You wyshed then out of the boke,
   But you were suer to haue in store   235   But you wished such things out of the Bible.
   Plentie of scripturs, euermore
To proue that you myght aye be bolde
Wyth your owne to do what you woulde.   238

You thought
you might em-
ploy your goods
in any way;
[Page 27]

"You thought you myght your goodis employ
   To priuate gayne in euery thynge.
You thought it no faute to anoye

Mat. vii.

   Such men as were nygh you dwellynge,   242
   Were it by purchaise or byldynge ;

that you might
annoy your
neighbour;

Neither to get into your hande,
Your neyghbours house his goodis and lande.   245

"All was your owne that you myght bye,
   Or for a long tyme take by lease ;
And then woulde you take rent yerely,

Luke .iii.

   Much more then was the tenantis ease :   249

that it was not
wrong to double
your rents.

   It was no faute your rentis to rease
From twentie markis to fourtie powndis,
   Were it in tenementis or growndis.   252

[Page 28]
If the poor did
die for want of
house and food,

"What though the pore dyd lye and dye
   For lacke of harboure, in that place
Where you had goten wyckedly
   By lease, or else by playne purchase,   256
   All houseynge that shoulde, in that case,
Haue ben a safegard [1] and defence
   Agaynst the stormy violence ?   259

you thought you
were blameless,

"Yea, what if the pore famyshed
   For lacke of fode vpon that grownde,

Math. x.

The rentes whereof you haue reysed,
   Or hedged it wythin your mownde ?   263
   There myght therwyth no faute be founde,

[Page 29]

No, though ye bought vp all the grayne
   To sell it at your pryce agayne.   266

and that I should
not require their
blood at your
hand.

"You thought that I woulde not requyre
   the bloude of all suche at your hande ;
But be you sure, eternall fyre
   Is redy for eche hell fyrebrande,   270
   Boeth for the housynge and the lande

Iacob. ii.

·That you haue taken from the pore
   Ye shall in hell dwell euermore !   273

           [1] Original, slafegard.

" Yea, that same lande that ye dyd take

    From the plowemen that laboured sore,

Causeynge them wycked shyftis to make,

    Shall nowe ly vpon you full sore ;   277

    You shal be damned for euermore :

The bloude of them that dyd amisse,

Through your defaute is cause of this.   280

The land taken from the plowman shall be a burden upon you,

[Page 30]

and sink you to hell.

Mat. xxiii.[1]

" The fathers, whose children dyd growe

    In idlenes to a full age,

Woulde fayne be excused by you

    That were the cause that they dyd rage ;   284

    You toke from them theyr heritage,

Leaueyng them nought wheron to worcke :

Which lacke dyd make them learne to lurke.   287

You took from children their heritage,

" The sones also, that wycked were,

    And wrought after theyr wycked wyll,

Would nowe ryght fayne be proued cleare,

    Bycause your mysse hath made them ille ;   291

    But they muste nedis be gyltie styll,

Because they woulde worke wyckedly,

Rather then lyue in miserie.   294

[Page 31]

and made them what they are ;

" And yet shall you answere for all,

    Theyr bloude I wyl of you require,

Because you were cause of theyr falle,

    That are become vesselles of ire ;   298

    Boeth they and you shall haue your hyre

In hell emonge that wycked sorte,

That lyue in paynes wythout conforte.   301

but you will answer for their ill deeds,

Ezech. iii.

[Page 32]

☞ " Infyne, all such as dyd amysse

    Through your defaut, what so they be,

Shall lyue in payne that endlesse is,

    Because they would not credite me,   305

    That am the trueth and verite.

I tolde them if they were opprest,

I woulde se all theyr wrongis redreste.   308

and for all who did amiss through you.

Hebru. xii.

    [1] xviii in original.

Rebels go to hell. "The wycked sorte, that dyd rebell
Agaynst you, when you dyd them wronge,
Shall haue theyr parte wyth you in hell,
Where you shall synge a dolefull songe :   312

[Page 33]   Worlde wythout ende you shall be stonge
Eccles. vii.   Wythe the pricke of the conscience :
A iuste rewarde for your offence.   315

You who are
guilty of simony
will go to hell.   ☞ " And you that woulde nedis take in hande
To guyde my flocke, as shepheardis shoulde,
Onlye to possesse rent and land,
·   And as much richesse as you coulde,   319
To leade your lyfe euen as you woulde,
Anoyde from me downe into hell,
Actu. viii.   Wyth Simon Magus there to dwell.   322

Your guilt
surpasses belief.   "If I should rehearse all at large
That in your wycked lyfe is founde,
[Page 34]   And laye it strayght to your charge,
No wyght there were in this world rownde   326
Genes. 7.   But woulde wonder I had not drownde
The hoole earth for your synne onlye,
That woulde be called my cleargie.   329

You made your
way into the fold
like wolves.   " Firste (wyth Magus) ye made your waye,
Lyke gredy woulves,[1] into my folde.
Your wycked wyll coulde fynde no staye
So longe as ought was to be solde,   333
Either for seruice or for golde :
By you the patrons fell from me,
And are become as ill as ye.   336

[Page 35]   ¶ " You dyd prouoke them fyrste to sell,
And then they learned forto bye ;
And made patrons
as bad as your-
selves.   Thynkynge that they myght bye as well
As the leadars of the clargie.   340
And then they founde meanes, by and by,
To catch, and kepe in theyr owne hande,
The tenth increase by sea and lande.   343

[1] woulles in original.

¶ "Theyr owne chyldren they dyd present,
   Theyr seruauntis, and theyr wycked kynne,
And put by such as I had sent
   To tell my people of theyr synne :   347
   And youe were gladde to take them in,
Bycause you knewe that they dyd knowe
That youe came in by the wyndowe.   350

They presented their children and servants.

Iohn .x.

[Page 36]

"Such as woulde haue entryd by me,
   That am the dore of my shepe folde,
You sayde were not worthy to be
   Admitted into my houscholde :   354
   You thought by them you should be tolde
Of your moste wycked Simonie,
Your falschead and your periurie.   357

Such as would have entered the fold by me were deemed unworthy.

Esaie. xex

¶ "You layde to theyr charge herecie,
   Sisme, and sedicion also ;
But you dyd them falsely belye,
   Thynckynge therby to worke them wo,   361
   And doubtlesse ofte it chaunced so :
For many of them you haue slayne
Wyth most extreme and bitter payne.   364

Act xxiiii

[Page 37]

Many of my servants you have slain.

¶ "Thus by your meanes my people haue
   Ben destitute of sheperdis good ;
They haue ben ledde by such as draue
   Them from the fylde of gostly foode ;   368
   They beate them backe wyth heauye mode,
And made them fede in morysh grownde,
Where neuer shepe coulde be fedde sownde.   371

¶ "The kyngis and rulars of the earthe,
   For lacke of knowledge, went astraye ;
And you stopped my seruantis breathe,
   That woulde haue taught them the ryght waye ;   375
   You thought your lyueynge woulde decaye,
If kyngis and rulars of the lande
Should theyr owne duitie vnderstande.   378

Kings have strayed for lack
[Page 38]
Apo, xviii of knowledge,

Iohn, xi.

but you are to
blame for this,

¶ " For so longe as you kept them blynde,
    Makynge them thyncke they had no charge,
You had all thyngis at your owne mynde,
    And made your owne powr wondrouse large.   382
    You had an owre in echmans barge ;
You bade the princis take no care,

[Page 39]
For you would all the dayngar beare.   385

and, having my
flock in your
hands,

¶ " This haueynge my flocke in your hande,
    You taught them not, but kept them blynde,
So that not one dyd vnderstande

Psal. xiiii.
    The lawes that I had lefte behynde.   389
    The maister could not teach his hynde
How he should worke in his callyng
Fearynge my wrath in euery thynge.   392

    " The father coulde not teach his sonne
    Howe, in his dayes, to walke vpryght ;

for the ignorance
of the people.
But gaue him leaue at large to runne
    In wycked wayes, booth daye and nyght,   396

[Page 40]
    Makyng him wycked in my syght :
O wycked guidis, this was your dede.

Ezech. iii
But I shall requite you your mede !   399

☞ " The matrons and mothers also,
    Coulde not teach theyr daughters my lawe,
But wyckedly they let them go
    Whyther theyre wycked luste dyd drawe :   403

You saw it all,
and are guilty
of all the faults
Can you denie but this you sawe ?
And whye dyd you not set them ryght
To seke thynges pleasante in my syght ?   406

☞ " All maner men were oute of frame ;
    None knewe his duitie thorowly ;

[Page 41]
Ier. xxiii
arising from
simony.
And you are founde in all the blame,
    That haue entred by Simonie ;   410
Whych thynge you shall dearely bye,
For wyth Satan you shall be sure,
Worlde without ende, styll to endure.   413

☞ " For at your handis nowe I requyre
   The bloude of all that perished
In placis were you toke the hyre,
   And let my flocke be famisshed.   417
For aye ye shal be banyshed
The blysse that I bought for them all
That folowed me when I dyd call.   420 *Iohn. x*

The blood of all who have perished is required at your hand,

" Auoyde from me downe into hell,
   All ye that haue wrought wyckedly :
wyth Lucifer there shall ye dwell,
   And lyue in paynes eternally.   424
Your wycked soule shall neuer nye,
But lyue in payne for euermore,
Because ye paste not for my lore.   427

[Page 42]

and you must dwell with Lucifer.

Mark, ix

" Awaye, awaye ye wycked sorte !
   Awaye, I saye, oute of my syght :
Henseforth you ¹sha[ll] haue no conforte,
   But bytter mournynge daye and nyght,   431
   Extreme darknes wythouten lyghte.
Wepynge, waylynge, wyth sobbynge sore,
Gnashyng of teeth for euermore,   434

Depart into darkness and sorrow, [Page 43] *Mat. xxv Luke .xiii.*

" Your conscience shall not be quiete,
   But shall styll burne lyke flameynge fyre ;
No burnyng brymston hath such heate
   As you shall haue for youre iuste hyre ;   438
   The hote vengeaunce of my greate ire
Shall be styll boylynge in your breaste,
So that you shall neuer take reste."   441

into the lake of fire and brimstone.

Then shall the wycked fall in haste
   Downe into the pyt bottomelesse ;
Moste bytter paynes there shall they taste,
   And lyue euer in greate distresse.   445
   None shall confort theyr heauinesse ;
In deadly paynes there shall they lye :
And then they would but shall not dye.   448

Mat. xiii.

[Page 44]

The wicked will then fall into hell,

Apocal. ix.

¹ (sh u)

¶ Such as were here so loth to dye,
 That they thought no ph[y]sicke to dere,
Shall there lyue in such miserie
  That only death myght their hertis chere.   452

where they shall
ever be wishing
to die.
They shall alwayes desyre to here
 That they myght dye for euermore,
Theyr paynes shal be so passynge sore.   455

Then shall Christe wyth his chosen sorte
[Page 45]
 Triumphauntely returne agayne
To hys Father, geueyng conforte
Apoc, xxii
[See Rev. xx, 4.]
 To such as for hys sake were slayne.   459
No wyght shall there fele any payne,
But all shall lyue in such blysse there,
 As neuer tonge coulde yet declare.   462

That we may live
with Christ in
heaven,
That we maye then lyue in that place,
 Wyth Christe oure kynge that hath vs bought,
Let vs crie vnto God for grace
  To repent that we haue mysse wrought ;   466
 And where we haue wyckedly sought
Luke .xix.
To be made rych by wycked gayne,
[Page 46]
 Let vs restore all thynges agayne.   469

let the poor man
enjoy his
copyhold;
Let the pore man haue and enioye
 The house he had by copycholde,
For hym, his wyfe, and Iacke hys boye,
  To kepe them from hunger and colde ;   473
 And thoughe the lease thereof be solde,
Bye it agayne though it be dere,
Phil. iiii.
For nowe we go on oure laste yere.   476

let the enclosures
be laid open
again ;
Caste downe the hedges and stronge mowndes,
 That you haue caused to be made
Aboute the waste and tyllage growndes,
  Makeynge them wepe that erste were glad ;   480
[Page 47]
 Leste you your selfes be stryken sadde,
When you shall se that Christe doeth drye
Apoc, xxi.
All teares from the oppressedis eye.   483

Restore the fynes, and eke the rent,
 That ye haue tane more then your due ;
Else certenly you shall be shent,
  When Christe shall your euidence view ; 487
 For then you shall fynde these wordes trew,
You are but stuardes of the lande,
That he betoke into your handes. 490

let all fines and rents be restored ;

Luke .xix,

And you that haue taken by lease
 Greate store of growndis or of houseyng,
Your lyueyng thereby to encrease,
  And to maynetayne you loyeterynge, 494
 Fall nowe to worcke for your lyueynge,
And let the lordes deale wyth theyr growndis
In territories, fieldes, and townes. 497

and let the leasemongers work for their living.
[Page 48]

ii. The. iii

You do but heape on you Gods ire,
 Whych doubtles you shall fele shortely,
In that you do so muche desyre
  The lease of eche mans house to bye. 501
 You study no mans wealth, pardye,
But all men se you do aduaunce
Your selfe by pore mens hynderaunce. 504

You only heap on yourselves the anger of God.

Esaic. v.

What though your liueing ly theron ?
 Shoulde you not geue them vp therfore ?
It is abhomination ;
  And doubtles God wyll plage it sore. 508
 Repent, I saye, and synne no more,
For nowe the daye is euen at hande
When you shall at your tryall stande. 511

[Page 49]

It is an abomination.

Let not the wealthy lyueynge here
 (Which can but a shorte tyme endure)
Be vnto you a thynge so dere
  That you wyll lose endlesse pleasure, 515
 Rather then leaue the vayne treasure.
O, rather let your leases go,
Then they shoulde worke you endelesse woe. 518

Repent, or else you will lose heaven.

[Page 50]

Restore the tithes,
that the poor,
the blind, and
the lame,

Restore[1] the tythes vnto the pore,
　　For blynde and lame shoulde lyue theron,
The wydowe that hath no succoure,
　　And the chylde that is lefte alone ;　　522
For if these folke do make theyr mone
To God, he wyll sure heare theyr crye,
And reuenge theyr wronge by and by.　　525

Restore your tythes, I saye, once more,
and true preach-
ers may lyve
thereon.
　　That tr[e]we preachars may lyue theron,
And haue all nedefull thynges in store
[Page 51]
　　To geue to such as can get none,　　529
Leste theyr greate lamentation
Do styr the Lorde vengeaunce to take,
Euen for hys trueth and promes sake.　　532

You, the men of
God, must give up
your pluralities.
Geue ouer your pluralities,
　　Ye men of God, if you be so ;
Betake you to one benifice,
　　And let your lordelyke lyueuynges go,　　536
For holy wryte teacheth you so.
Learne at the laste to be content
Wyth thynges that be sufficient.　　539

If you be mete to do seruice
[Page 52]
　　To any prince or noble man,
Than medle wyth no benifice ;
You cannot do
two men's work.
　　For certenly no one man can　　543
　　Do the duitie of moe men than
Of one : which duitie you do owe
To them that geue you wage, you knowe.　　546

Rob the people
no more.
☞ Robbe not the people that do paye
　　The tenth of theyr increase yerely,
To haue a learned guyde alwaye .
　　Present wyth them to edifie　　550
Them by teachyng the veritie,
Malac. iii
Booth in his worde and eke his dede,
[Page 53]
And to succoure such as haue nede.　　553

　　　　　　　　[1] Rehore in original.

☞ And you that haue tane vsurie You that have
taken usury,
make restitution.
  Of such as nede draue to borowe,
Make restitution shortly,
  Leste it turne you to great sorowe, 557
  When no man can be your borowe, *Psal xv.*
[See Psal. xlix. 7.]
Wich shal be at the daye of dome ; *Phil. iiii.*
Which doubtlesse is not longe to come. 560

☞ And you that by disceyte haue wonne,[1] [1 Orig. wome.] You that have
deceived,
  Were it in weyght or in measure, be sorry and
make recom-
Be sorye that ye haue so donne, pense.
  And seke to stoppe Goddis displeasure, 564
  By bestowynge this worldis treasure [Page 54]
Luke. iii
To the confort, helpe, and succoure
Of such as be nedie and pore. 567

¶ And you that erste haue bene oppreste, You who have
rebelled, repent
  And could not beare it paciently, heartily.
For you I thynke it shalbe beste
  To repent you must hertily, 571
  And call to God for his mercie,
To geue you grace forto sustayne
That crosse when it shall come agayne. 574 *Marc.* 14

To make an ende—let vs repent Let all repent,
and pray God
  All that euer we haue mysse wrought, for mercy.
And praye to God omnipotent [Page 55]
  To take from vs all wycked thought, 578
  That his glory maye be styll sought
By vs that be his creatures,
So longe as lyfe in vs endures. 581

And that henceforth eche man maye seke And let each man
seek the good of
  In all thyngis to profite all men, others.
And be in herte lowly and meke,
  As men that be in dede Christen, 585
  As well in herte as name ; and then
We shall haue blysse wythouten ende :
Unto the which the Lorde vs sende. 588
Amen.

[Page 56, blank]

[Page 57] ## The Boke to the Christian Readars.

The "Trumpet" warned all to walk uprightly.

MY brother (the Trumpet) dyd warne you before,
 That al men shuld walk in their callynge vp-
ryght,
Directyng their wayes by Gooddis holy lore,
 knowyng that thei be always in the Lordis syght.
 Whoe seeth in the darcke as well as in lyght.
He hath cryed vnto you all this last yere,
And yet non emendment doeth in you appeare.   595

God is welcome to some men, but they seem to disdain His warnings.

In dede, very many do him entertayne
 Lyke as there were none more welcome then he.
Yet I thyncke they do his warnynge dysdayne,
 Because he doeth tell them *what is theyr duetie,
 For he is very playne wyth euery degre :
The rych and the myghtie he doeth nothyng feare,
No more doeth he wyth the pore mans falte beare. 602

[* Page 58]

The "Trumpet" was sent to pre- pare His way,

It pleased my father to sende him before,
 That he myght make redy and prepare his waye,
By causeynge all men to walke in his lore,
 That haue in tymes passed wandred astraye,   606
 Leste payne be theyr portion at the laste daye.

and now I come that men may see, as in a glass, what their reward shall be.

And nowe hath he sent me that they maye se,
As it were in a glasse, what theyr rewarde shal be :
I am the rewarde that al men shall haue,
 For the iuste shall haue plesure and the wicked
payne.[1]

[Page 59]

When euery man shal aryse oute of his graue,
 And haue the spryte knyt to the body agayne,   613
 In heauen or in hell they shall styll remayne :
Of blysse or of payne they shall haue theyr fyll—
The good sorte in heauen, and in hell the ill.   616

[1] panye in original.

Beholde me, therfore, wyth a gostly eie,

   And let me not from your presence departe ;

For no doubt you wyll all wyckednes defye.

   So longe as I shall remayne in your herte,   620

   I shall cause you from wyckednes to conuert,

So that, in the ende, you shalbe ryght sure

To lyue wyth my father in ioye and pleasure.   623

Behold me, therefore, and let me not depart from your presence.

Finis.

¶ Imprin-
ted at london by Robert
Crowley dwellynge
in Elie rentis in
Holburne
Anno Domini
.M. D. L. I.

[Page 60]

[front leaf] ¶ **The Way to**

Wealth, wherein is plain-

ly taught a most present Remedy

for Sedicion. Wrytten and imprinted

by Robert Crowley the .viii. of

February in the yere of

our LORDE.

A thousand fiue

hunderd & fif-

tie

(∴)

☞ In Elie Rentes in

Holburne

¶ Cum priuilegio ad impri=

mendum solum.

☞ Who so thou be that doest desyre,
To liue and good dayes se,
Toke *that* in thy tonge and thy lyps,
None yl or disceite be.
Fle from yl and do that good is,
Whereof commeth no blame,
Seke thou for peace diligently,
And then ensue the same.

Psalm xxxiiii.

[Blank page.]

¶ By what meanes se=
dicion maye be put a=waye, and

what distruction wil folow if it be

not put away spedely.

Consultatio Robert

Crolet .·.

Conside=

ring that al men maye playnely perceiue the
greate hurte *that* (of late daies) Sedicion hath
done in thys realme, & that all wyse men maye
esilye gather what greater hurte is lyke to
ensue, if it be not spedely sene vnto, it shalbe euery 5
true Englyshmans duty forth-wyth to employe his
whole study to the remouyng of so great an euel oute
of so noble a realme and commone wealth ; leste, haply
(if throughe negligence it growe and take deper rote)
it be shortly to stronge and more suerly grounded than
that it maye be rooted oute wythoute the vtter destruction of the whole realme. For what can be more
true then that whych the Trueth it-selfe hath spoken ? 13
"Euery kyngdome " (sayeth Christe) "that *is deuided
in it-selfe shall be broughte to nought." Intendynge,
therefore, to playe the parte of a true Englyshman, and
to do all that in me shall ly to plucke thys stincking
wede vp by the rote, I shal in thys good busines do as,
in their euell exercise, the dise-playars (that gladlye 19
woulde, but haue nothynge to playe for) do :—Holde
the candle to them that haue wherewyth, and wyll
sette lustily to it. And so doyng, I shal be no lesse
worthy the name of a true herted Englishman then
the trumpettar is worthy *the* name of a man of war,
thoughe he do not in dede fyght, but animate and
encourage other. 26

Sedition therfore, beinge a daungerous disease in
the bodie of a commen-wealth, muste be cured as the
expert Phisicians do vse to cure the daungerous diseases
in a naturall bodie. And as the moste substanciall
waye in curinge diseases is by puttinge awaye the 31
causes wherof they grewe, so is it in the pullinge vp of
Sedition. For if the cause be once taken awaye, then
muste the effecte nedes faile. If the rote be cut of the

Margin notes:
Considering what sedition has done, it is a duty to see what can be done to remove the evil out of this noble realm;

because if let alone it may take such deep root, that it may be the ruin of the kingdom.

Mathew .xii.
[* A ii, back!]

Intending to act as a true English-man, and to do all I can to re-move so stinking a weed,

I shall hold the candle to those who can and will remedy the mat-ter, and so shall be no less worthy the name of Englishman than a trumpeter that of man of war.

Sedition is a disease, and must be cured, as physicians cure the dangerous diseases of the natural body,

by putting away the cause. If the root be cut

---

¹ There are 32 pages. The signatures *marked* are these,
A .ii., B .i., B .ii., B .iii., B .iiii. "An° 1550" is written on title.

braunch must nedes die. The boughes cannot budde
if the tree haue no sappe.

37   Geue eare therfore (O my countrey-men) geue eare !

And do not disdaine to heare the aduise of one of the
leaste of youre brethren, *for the matter requireth euerie
mans counsell, and God reueiled vnto younge Daniell
that whiche the whole counsell of Babilon perceiued

not. Geue eare, I saye, and if I tell you trueth, be
not ashamed to do *that* I bid, thoughe ye knowe me to
be at youre commaundement. For Abraham was contented to do at the biddinge of Saraie his wife, because

he knewe that hir biddinge was Gods will. And tho
Niniuites did, at the biddinge of pore Ionas, sit in
sackecloth & ashes, because they perceiued that he

tolde them the trueth. Yea, cruell Herode did not
refuse to heare Iohn Baptiste, because the thinge
whiche he told him was true. Leaste you therfore
shulde be more loftie then the Babilonians, more
shamefast then Abraham, more stubborne then the
Niniuites, & more cruell then Herod, geue eare,[1] and
patientlye heare what I shal saye !   55

The causes of Sedition muste be roted oute. If I
shuld demaunde of the pore man of the contrey what
thinge he thinketh to be the cause of Sedition, I know
his answere. He woulde tel me that the great ferm-
ares, the grasiers, the riche buchares[2], the men of lawe,
the marchauntes, the gentlemen, the knightes, the

lordes, and I can not tel who ; men that haue no name
because they are †doares in al thinges that ani gaine
hangeth vpon. Men without conscience. Men vtterly
voide of Goddes feare. Yea, men that liue as thoughe
there were no God at all ! Men *that* would haue all in
their owne handes ; men that would leaue nothyng for
others ; men that would be alone on the earth ; men
that bee neuer satisfied. Cormerauntes, gredye gulles ;
yea, men that would eate vp menne, women, & chyldren,
are the causes of Sedition ! They take our houses ouer

our headdes, they bye our growndes out of our handes, they reyse our rentes, they leauie great (yea vnreasonable) fines, they enclose oure commens! No custome, no lawe or statute can kepe them from oppressyng vs in such sorte, that we knowe not whyche waye to turne vs to lyue. Very nede therefore constrayneth vs to stand vp agaynst them! In the countrey we can not tarye, but we must be theyr slaues and laboure tyll our hertes brast, and then they must haue al. And to go to the cities we haue no hope, for there we heare that these vnsaciable beastes haue all in theyr handes. Some haue purchased, and some taken by leases, whole allyes, whole rentes, whole rowes, yea whole streats 84 and lanes, so that the rentes be reysed, some double, some triple, and some four fould to that *they were wythin these .xii. yeres last past. Yea, ther is not so much as a garden grownd fre from them. No remedye 88 therfore, we must nedes fight it out, or else be brought to the lyke slauery that the French men are in! These idle bealies wil deuour al that we shal get by our sore labour in our youth, and when we shal be old and impotent, then shal we be driuen to begge and craue of them that wyl not geue vs so muche as the crowmes that fall from their tables. Such is the pytie we se in them! Better it were therfore, for vs to dye lyke men, then after so great misery in youth to dye more miserably in age! 98

Alasse, poore man, it pitieth me to se the myserable estate that thou arte in! Both for that thou arte so oppressed of them by whom thou shouldest be defended from oppression, and also for that thou knowest not thy dutye in thys great misery. Thow art not so much oppressed on the one side, but thou art more destituted 104 on the other syde. They that should norish and defend thy body in thy labour, do oppresse the; & they that shuld fede thy soule & strengthen thy mind to beare al this paciently, do leaue that alone. If thy

If your shepherd had been diligent

[* A iv, back]

112

the wolf might have come in nine sheepskins and not have deceived you.

You wouldn't have been persuaded you could prevail against the sword.

119

To revenge wrongs is, in a subject, to usurp the king's office, for the king is God's minister, to revenge the wrongs done to the innocent.

126

Christ would never go beyond the bounds of a private man, as *Luke .xii.* was seen when He was asked about the inheritance,

133

and in the matter of the woman taken in adultery.

[† A v]

137

If you had known all this, and had *John .xiii.* remembered other examples, *Numeri .xvi.* you would have *ii. Reg. xviii.* allowed yourselves to be torn in pieces rather than rebel against the king.

shepherde had bene a diligent watchman, & had espied the woulfe comyng vpon the, before *thou* hadst bene wit*h*in his reach, he wold haue stepped *betwene *th*e & th*ī*ne enemi, & enstructed *th*e in such sort, *that*, though he had come in nine shepe skinnes, yet he shoulde not haue deceiued thy syghte. The deuell shoulde neuer haue perswaded the *that* thou myghtest reuenge thyne owne wronge! The false prophetes shoulde neuer haue caused the to beleue that thou shouldeste preuaile againste them with the swerde, vnder whose gouernaunce God hath apointed the to be. He would haue told the that to reuenge wronges is, in a subiect, to take and vsurpe the office of a kinge, and, consequently, the office of God. For the king is Goddes minister to reuenge the wronges done vnto the innocent. As he that taketh in hande, therefore, or presumeth to do anye office vnder a kinge, not beinge lawfully called vnto it, presumeth to do the office of a kinge, so he that taketh in hand to do the office of a king, taketh Goddes office in hand.

We reade that oure Sauioure Christ, beinge in the estimation of the worlde but a priuate man, wold not walke out of the boundes of that vocacion. But when a certaine ma*n* came vnto him & desired that he would comma*u*nd hys brother to deuide the enheritau*n*ce wyth him, he axed who had appointed him to be iudge in suche matters? And againe, when the woman take*n* in adultery was broughte vnto hym, he shoulde not geue sentence †of the lawe against her, but axed hir if any man had condemned hir, and vpon hir deniall let hir go. If these examples, with the terrible stories of Corah, Datha*n*, Abira[m] and Absolom had ben diligently beate*n* into thine heade, thou wouldeste (no doubte) haue quieted thy selfe, and haue suffered thy selfe rather to haue bene spoyled of altogether, yea, and thy bodie toren in peces, rather the*n* thou wouldest haue taken on the more then thou art

called vnto. For no cause can be so greet to make it 145
lawful for the to do againste Goddes ordinaunce. But
thy shepeherde hathe bene negligent, as (alas the
while !) all shepcherdes be at this daie, and hath not
enstructed the aright. He espied not the wolf before
he had woried the, or happlye he knewe him not frome 150
a shepe. But it is moste like he was but an hirelinge,
and cared for no more but to be fedde with the milcke
& fatlinges and cladde with the woule, as the greateste
numbre of them that beare the name of shepeherde in
Englande be at this daie. Yea, perchaunce he had
many flockes to kepe, & ther-fore was absent from them
al, leauing with euerye flocke a dogge that woulde
rather worye a shepe then driue away the woulfe. 158

Wel, brother, these be greate plages, & it behoueth
the synnes to be greate that haue *deserued these so
great and intollerable plages at Goddes hande. Returne
to thi conscience therfore, and se if thou haue not deserued all this, and more to. Consider, firste, if thou
haue loued thy neighboure as thy self ; consider if thou
haue done nothing vnto him that thou wouldeste not
that he shoulde do vnto the. Loke if thou haue not
gone about to preuent him in any bargen that thou
hast sene him about ; loke if thou haue not craftely
vndermined him to get some thing out of his hand, or
to deceiue him in some bargein. Loke if thou haue
not laboured him oute of his house or ground. Se if 171
thou haue not accused him falsely or of malice, or else
geuen false euidence againste him. Se if thou haue not
geuen euell counsell to his wife or seruauntes, which
might turne him to displeasure. Consider if thou haue
not desired and wished in thine herte to haue his commoditie from him if thou mightest, without blame of
the worlde, haue broughte it aboute. For God loketh
vpon the herte, and if thine herte haue bene infected
with ani of these euilles, then haste thou bene abomin-

But all shepherds
are negligent at
this day,

and yours was,
perhaps, a
hireling, and
only cared to be
fed and clothed,
as the greatest
number do.

Perhaps he had
many flocks to
keep, and left a
dog with every
one, that would
rather worry the
sheep than drive
away the wolf.
These are great
plagues, and
[* A v, back]
your sins must
have been great
to deserve them.
See if you haven't
deserved them.
Have you loved
your neighbour
as yourself, and
done nothing
unto him that
you wouldn't do
to yourself?
Never tried to
overreach him
in a bargain?
Have you not
deceived him in
many things?
Have you not
accused him
falsely, or of
malice?
given false
evidence against
him?
Have you not
coveted his
goods?
And wouldn't
you have brought
it about if you
could without
blame?
God looks on the
heart, and if you

have done this you are abominable in His sight, and have deserved punishment.

able in the sight of God, and haste deserued these plages at Goddes hand.　　　　182

Now if you be found abhominable in thy behauioure towardes thy neighboure what shalt thou be founde, trowest thou, in *thy demaners to God ward? God requireth thine whole hert, thyne whole mynd, and al the powers of thy body and soule. "Thou shalt loue thy Lord God wyth all thy lyfe, wyth al thy mynd, and wyth al thy strength." That is to say, ther shal be nothynge in the whych thou shalt not apply wholly to the loue of thy Lord God. But how was it possible for the to loue God (whom thou seest not), syth thou louest not thy brother whom thou seest? God requireth the to loue him euer,

And if you are abominable in [* A vi] your behaviour to your neighbour, how do you stand in God's sight? God requires Math. xxii. your whole heart, mind, and body, and how could you love Him if you loved not your brother?

194　and how often hast thou gone whole dayes togither, whole weakes, yea whole yeres, and neuer thought once to loue hym aryght? How many and how great benefites hast thou receyued at Goddes hand, and howe vnthanckful hast thou bene for them, thynckynge that thou haste gotten them by thyne owne laboure and not receyued them frely at Goddes hand? As though God had not geuen the thy lyfe, thyne health, and thy strength to laboure! Yea, and as thoughe it were not

How many benefits have you received and been vnthankful, and thought you had won them by your own power, as though God had not given them to you?

203　God only that geueth the increase of euerye mans labour. But knowynge by thyne owne creacion and bryngyng vp, and also by the yonge fruite that God sendeth *the* of thy bodi, & further by the frutes *that* God sendeth, and causeth yerely to growe out of *the* earth, *that* there is a God Almyghty. Yet *thou* hast †not honoured him as God, but hast turned the glorie of God into an image made after the shape, or similitude, of mortall man ; renninge and ridinge from place to place to seke and to honoure thinges of thine owne makeinge ; crienge and callinge vpon them in thy nede and paying vnto them thy vowes, and thancking them for thyne health receiued ; doinge them dayly worshipe

By His works you know there is a God. Yet you have not [† A vi, back] honoured Him, Romaynes .i. but have turned His glory into an image like to man, and have gone from place to place to honour a thing of your own making.

216　and reuerence in the temples, and bestowinge thine

almes vpon them in deckinge them and setting lightes
before them! Biside this thou haste put confidence of
saluacion in pardones that *thou* haste bought, in prayers
that thou hast hiered, or mumbled vp thy selfe, in
Masses that thou hast caused to be saide, and in
worckes that thou thy selfe haste fantasied; and haste
not thanckefullye receyued the free mercye of God
offered vnto the in Christ, in whom onlye thou maiste
haue remission of thy sinnes! And therfore God hath
geuen the vp in to a reprobate minde to do the thinge
that is not beseminge. Euen to stande vp againste
God and Goddes ordinaunce, to refuse his Holy Word,
to delite in lies and false fables, to credite false prophetes, and to take weapen in hand against Goddes
chosen ministers: I saye his chosen ministers, for be
they good or bad, they are Goddes chosen, if they be
*good, to defende the innocente, if they be cuell, to
plage the wicked. If thou wilt therfore that God shall
deliuer the or thy children from the tirannie of them
that oppresse the, lament thine olde sinnes, and endeuour emendment of life. And then he that caused
King Cirus to send the Iewes home to Ierusalem
againe, shall also stire vp our yong king Edward to
restore the to thy liberty againe, and to geue straight
charge that non shalbe so bolde as once to vexe or trouble
the. "For the herte of a kinge is in Goddes hand, &
as he turneth the riuers of water, so turneth he it."

Be sure therfore, that if thou kepe thy selfe in
obedience and suffer al this oppression patiently, not
geueing credite vn to false prophecies that tel the of
victori, but to the worde of God that telleth the thy
dutie; thou shalt at the time, and after the maner that
God hath alredie pointed, be deliuered. Perchaunce
God wyl take from thine oppressours their hard stony
hertes, & geue them hertes of fleshe; for it is in hys
power so to do. Let him alone therfore. Reade the

Side notes:

217

You have put your trust for salvation in pardons which you have bought, and in masses which you have caused to be said, and in works which you have imagined.

So God has given you up to a reprobate mind,

Rom. i.

to refuse His word, to delight in lies and fables, believe false prophets, and to rebel against His ministers.

232

[* A vii]

If you wish to be delivered from oppression you must lament your sins, and strive to amend

i. Esdras .i.

your manner of living,

Then King Edward will give liberty again, and give command that none shall oppress you.
Prouerb .xxi.

243

Be obedient, and suffer patiently, giving no ear to false prophecies which speak of victory, but listen to God,

Ezech. xi.

and in the end you shall be delivered from all your oppressors,

252

Reade Iere-
mie hys pro-
phecie.
and learn your
duty in cap-
[* A vii, back]
tivity, how vain
to believe pro-
phecies of victory
if you deserve
captivity.

prophecie of Ieremie, and especially the seuen and
twentie Chapter, the eighte and twentie and the nine
and twenti, and therein thou shalte learne thy ductie
in captiuitye, and howe vayne a thynge it is to *credite
the prophetes that prophecie vyctorie to theym that
haue, by their synnes, deserued to be led awaye cap-
tyue, yea, and to remaine captiue till suche time as the

260 time be complete duringe whiche God hath determined

If you are still
stubborn, God
will make you
stoop : and if
your rulers are
too weak He will
bring strangers
in to subdue you.

to punishe them. And know thou for certentie, that if
thou be stil stouberne, God wil not leaue the so. He
will bringe the on thy knees; he wyl make the stoupe !
If the *gentlemen* and rulars of thy countreic shoulde be
to weake for the, he would bringe in strainge nations

266 to subdue the (as the Babilonians did the Iewes) and
leade the away captiue. So that, refusing to serue in
thine own countrie, thou shalte be made a slaue in a

Don't strive
against the
stream—
it is all for your
sins that you
suffer this op-
pression.
God has sent it,
and you must
bear it:
let it not be in
vain, let it do
what He intended
it should do; and
if you repent you
will become a
new man.

strainge contrei. Quiet thy selfe therfore, & striue not
againste the streame. For thi sinnes haue deserued
this oppression, and God hath sent it the as a iust rewarde for thy sinnes; & be *thou* neuer so loth, yet
nedes sustaine it thou muste. Apointe thy selfe therfore
to beare it. Let it not be layed vpon the in vain; let
it do the thing *that* God hath sent it for; let it cause
the to acknowledge thy sinne, repent it, and become
altogether a new man. That in the day when God
shall deliuer the, his name maie be glorified in the.

Then you shall
have true pro-
phets,

[† A viii]

And then God shal send *the* plentie of true prophets,
that shal go before *the* in puriti of life and godli doctrine. †They shal not come or send .iiii. times in an

282 yere and no more; neyther shal they set one to gather

who will not
leave you desti-
tute of a diligent
guide, as your
shepherds do
now-a-days.

vp the tenth of thyne encrease to their behoufe, and
leaue the destitute of a diligente guyde (as thy shepherdes do nowe a dayes)! But God hath promised by
hys prophete to take awaye these shepeherdes from the,
and to commyt the to the kepynge of Dauid hys fayeth-

288 ful seruaunte; that is to saye, to such as wyll be as

diligent in feadyng the, as Dauid was in gouernyng the 289
people of whom he had gouernaunce.

289

Geue care therfore ye shephardes of thys church of
Englande! Ye Byshoppes, ye Deanes, Archdiacons and
Canons; ye Persons and ye Vicares, what soeuer ye be,
that receyue any parte of the tenth of mens yerelye encrease, or any other patrimony of preachers, geue eare to
the prophet Ezechiel! For *the* same Lord *that* bad him
speake vnto *the* sheperdes of Iuda, byddeth hym speake
vnto you nowe also. " Thou sonne of manne," sayth the 298
Lord, " prophecye agaynst the shepherdes of England,
prophecy and say vnto those shepheardes :—thus sayeth
the Lord God : Wo be to the shepherdes of England,
that haue fed them selues! What ought not those
shepherdes to haue fed those flockes of England ? Ye
eate the fatte, aud decke youre selues * with the woule,
& the mutton that is fat ye kil to fede vpon, but these
silli shepe ye fede not. The soroweful & pensiue ye
haue not comforted, the sicke ye haue not healed, *the*
broken ye haue not bound vp, the stray shepe ye haue
not brought againe nor sought for *the* lost. But *with*
extreme crueltie ye haue plaied the lordes ouer them,
&c." I nede not to reherse more of this prophets
saiyng vnto you, for ye know where to haue it, and
haue leysure inough to seke it, for ought that I se you
busied withal; onlesse it be with purchaisinge landes
for youre heires, & finde fingered ladies, whose woman-
like behauiour and motherlike housewifry ought to be
a lighte to al women that dwell aboute you, but is so
fare otherwise, that, vnlesse ye leaue them landes to
marye them wythall, no man wyll set a pinne by them
when you be gone. Wel, loke to this geare be tyme, 320
leaste perhappes it brede a scabbe emonge you.

I woulde not your wiues shoulde be taken from you.
but I wold you shoulde kepe them to the furtheraunce
of Goddes trueth, wherof ye professe to be teacheares.

Give ear, ye bishops, deans, archdeacons, parsons, and vicars, whatso-ever you are, who receive tenths of men's yearly increase, to the Prophet Ezekiel, whom God has commanded to speak to you.

298

Ezech. xxxiiii. " Woe to the shepherds of England, who have fed them-[* A viii, back] selves. You eat the fat, and wear the wool, and kill the best, but these sheep you feed not. The sorrowful you have not comforted ; the sick you have not healed ; the broken you have not bound up ; the straying you have not re-covered. But with extreme cruelty you have played the lords over God's heritage." *Nota bene how prystes wyves ought [t]o behaue them selfes &c. &c.*

320
I would not take your wives from you, but I would have them kept to further God's truth, whereof you profess to be teachers ;

325 Let youre wiues therefore put of theire fine frockes and
Frenche hoodes, & furnishe them selues with al pointes

that they may be
a help, and not a
[* B i]
hindrance.
i. Timo. iii.

of honest housewifery, and so let them be an helpe to
youre studie and not a lette. S. Paul teacheth *you
not to make them ladies or gentlewomen. Neither
doeth he teache you to be so gredie vpon liueings, that,

331 for the liueinge sake, ye will take vpon you the dueties
of twentie men, and yet do not the duetie of one ; no,
some of you be not able to do anye part of one dutie !

If God's word
allow you to
hold divers
offices in divers
places, to be a
dean in one, a
canon in another,
a parson here,
and a parson
there,
set your pens to
paper, and prove
it, and we will
aid you all in
our power.
If you can't do
this, give over
your pluralities,
and be content
with one living,
and do your duty,

If Goddes Worde do alow it that one of you shulde be
a deane in one place, a canone in an other, a parsone
here and a parsone there, a Maister of an house in
Oxforde or Cambridge and an officer in the kinges
house, and yet to do none of the duities herof thorowly ;
then set your pennes to the paper, and satisfie vs bi
Goddes Word, and we wil also helpe you to oure
power to satisfie the consciences of them that be offended at youre doinges herin. If you can not do so,
then geue ouer youre pluralities and make your vnsaciable desires geue place to Goddes trueth. Content
your selfe with one competent liueinge, and faile not to

346 be diligente in doinge the duetie therof. But if ye

or you will hear
more of it.
Your checking
of one or two
men in a corner
can't stop every
man's mouth in
a matter of
truth.

wyll do neither of boeth, truste to it ye shall heare
more of it ! Youre checkinge of one or two in a corner
can not stop euerye mannes mouth in a matter of
trueth, beynge so great an infamie to the Gospel of
God which ye professe. And if ye wil nedes hold

352 stil your pluralities for your lordlike liueing sake, doubt

[† B i, back]

†ye not ye wyll be charged with that whiche ye woulde

Your unworthy
curates have
stirred up the
people in the
late tumults.

seme to be cleare of. For a great numbre of youre
vnworthye curates haue bene the stirrars vp of the
simple people in the late tumultes that haue bene ;

357 where as if you had not robbed them of that which

Where they had
a godly teacher
the people were
quiet.

thei paye yearely to haue a learned and Godly teacher,
they had bene better enstructed, as appeared by the quietnes that was emonge them that had such shepeherdes.

Well, brother, thou, I saie, that art thus oppressed on the one side and destituted on the other, take mine aduise with the. Submit thy self wholy to the wyll of God. Do thy laboure truly, cal vpon God continually. I meane not that thou shuldest be euer muttering on thy beads, or *that* thou shouldest haue any beads, but my meaninge is, that thou shouldest euer haue thine harte lifted vp vnto God ; for so meaneth Sainte Paul when he sayeth, " I would men should pray alwayes, and in all places, liftinge vp theire pure handes, &c." And in all thy doinges let thy desire be that Goddes wil be fulfilled in the, and what so euer God sendeth the, holde the content wit*h*al, and render vnto him most hertie than*c*kes, for that he dealeth so mercifully with the ; acknowledginge that bi his iustice 375 he might poure oute vpon the mo plages then euer * were heard of. And, when thou commeste to thy parishe church, if thy cur[a]te be an euell liuear, then remember what Christe said vn to his disciples :—" When the Scribes and Pharises do set them downe vpon Moses seate, then do al that they commaunde you to do, but 381 do not as they do ; for they say & do not." Remember this, I saie, and what so euer thi curate biddeth the do when he sitteth on Christes seate, that is, when he readeth the Bible vnto the, that do thou. But folowe not his examples ! Do not as thou seest him do ; but at thy firste entraunce into the church, lifte vp thine herte vnto God, and desire of hym that he wyll geue the his Holye Spirit to illumine and lighten the eies of 389 thine herte, that thou maist se and perceiue the true meaning of all the Scriptures that thou shalte heare reade vnto the that dai. And so shalt thou be sure, that thoughe thy curate were a deuell, and would not that any man shoulde be the better for that whiche he readeth, yet thou shalt be edified, and learne as much as shalbe necessarye for thy saluacion. And for thy

1 2

necessary for you, and for your sake your curate shall speake plainly, so that you can under-
Actu. ii.
stand him.
[* B ii, back]
402

If you are de-sirous to learn your duty, God will make it plain.

He made the He-brew tongue plain to all men on the day of Pentecost.
409

Thus you see the cause of sedition is not where you lay it, but your own sin is the cause. Sedition is let loose upon you to plague you for your sins.
418

If I demand of the "greedy cor-morants" what they think is the cause, they will answer,
" Peasant knaves are too wealthy ; provender pricks
[† B iii]
them ;
they regard no laws ;
they would have all things in common ;
would fix our rents ;

cast down our parks ; lay our pastures open ;

sake God shall make thy curate (that otherwise wold mumble in the mouth & drounde his wordes) to speake out plainly, or else he shall geue the such a gift that thou shalt vnderstande him plainely. Of suche power is *God, for when the Apostles spake in the Hebrue tonge onlye al that were present heard euery man his own language. Doubt thou not therfore but if thou be desirous to learne thy duetie out of that thy curate readeth to the, God wil make it plaine vnto *the*, though it be not plainlye reade. For he that coulde make the Hebrue tonge (which sowndeth far otherwise then other tonges do) sownd al maner of languages, to euerie man his owne language, can also make thine owne language sownde plaine vnto the, though it were not spoken anye thinge plaine.

Thus seeste thou that the cause of Sedition is not where thou laiest it, for I haue declared to the that thine owne sinne is the cause that thou arte sedicious. For Sedition is poured vpon the to plage thy former sinne withall. Because thou knewest God bi his creatures and yet didest not honoure him as God, he hath geuen the ouer into a reprobate sence, to do the thinge that is vnsemelye, euen to stande vp againste God and Goddes ordinaunce, as I haue sayde before !

Nowe if I should demaund of the gredie cormer-auntes what thei thinke shuld be the cause of Sedition, they would saie :—"The paisant knaues be to welthy, prouender pricketh them ! They knowe not them selues, they knowe no obedience, they regard no lawes, thei would † haue no gentlemen, thei wold haue al men like themselues, they would haue al thinges commune ! Thei would not haue vs maisters of that which is our owne ! They wil appoint vs what rent we shal take for our groundes ! We must not make the beste of oure owne ! These are ioly felowes ! Thei wil caste doune our parckes, & laie our pastures open ! Thei wil haue

the law in their own ha*n*des! They wil play the kinges! They wyll compel the kinge to grau*n*t theyr requestes! But as they like their fare at *the* breakefaste they had this laste somer, so let the*m* do againe. They haue ben metely well coled, and shalbe yet better coled if they quiet not the*m* selues. We wyll tech the*m* to know theyr betters. And because they wold 439
haue al co*m*mone, we wil leaue the*m* nothing. And if they once stirre againe, or do but once cluster togither, we wil hang the*m* at their own dores! Shal we suffer *the* vilaines to disproue our doynges? No, we wil be lordes of our own & vse it as we shal thinke good!

and have the law in their own hands.

They liked the breakfast they had last summer; they were well cooled then.

We will leave them nothing.

We will hang them at their own doors. We'll do as we like with our own."

Oh good maisters, what shuld I cal you? You *that* haue no name, you *that* haue so many occupacio*n*s & trads *that* ther is no on name mete for you! You vnge*n*tle gentleme*n*! You churles chikens, I say! 448
Geue me leue to make answere for the pore ideotes ouer whom ye triumphe in this sorte. And this one thing I shal desire of you that ye report me not to *be one that fauoureth their euel doinges (for I take God to witnes I hate boeth theyre euell doinges and youres also), but geue me leaue to tel you as frely of your faultes, as I haue alreadi told them of theires. And for asmuch as you be stronge and they weake, I shall 456
desire you to beare with me though I be more ernest in rebuking your faultes, then I was in rebuking theirs.

What shall I call you, you ungentle gentlemen, you churl's chickens?

I will answer for these poor idiots.

[* B iii, back]

Don't say I favour their evil doings—I hate them and yours also.

Allow me to tell you your faults.

True it is, the pore men (who*m* ye cal paisaunte knaues) haue deserued more the*n* you can deuise to laie vpon them. And if euerye one of them were able and shoulde sustaine as much punishment as thei al 463
were able to sustaine, yet could thei not sustaine the plages *that* thei haue deserued. But yet if their offence wer laied in an equall balaunce with yours (as no doubt thei are in *the* sight [of] God) doubt not but you should sone be ashamed of youre parte. For what can you

True, the poor have deserved more than you can lay upon them,

but if their offence were put in an equal balance with yours, you would soon be ashamed.

469 laye vnto their charge, but they haue had examples of

Are they dis-
obedient? you
were first dis-
obedient,

the same in you? If you charge them wyth disobedience, you were firste disobedient. For without a law

473 to beare you, yea contrarie to the law which forbiddeth al maner of oppression & extortion, & that more is contrarie to conscience, the ground of al good lawes, ye

in enclosing the
commons, con-
[* B iv]
trary to law, in
levying greater
fines than here-
tofore, and in
raising rents.
When a law was
passed against
such things, you
compelled your
tenants to con-
sent to your
wishes.

enclosed frome the pore theire due commones, leauied greater fines then heretofore *haue bene leauied, put them from the liberties (and in a maner enheritaunce) that they held by custome, & reised theire rentes. Yea, when ther was a law ratified to the contrary, you ceased not to finde meanes either to compel your tenantes to consent to your desire in enclosinge, or else ye found such maistership that no man durste gaine saye your doinges for feare of displeasure. And

Where was your
obedience to the
proclamation for
laying open the
enclosures?

what obedience shewed you, when the kinges proclamations were sent forthe, and commissions directed for the laying open of your enclosures, and yet you lefte

What obedience
did you give to
the second pro-
clamation issued
by the king,
concerning the
contempt of his
laws?

not of to enclose stil? Yea, what obedience was this which ye shewed at such time as the kinges moste honourable counsell, perceiueinge the grudginge that was emong the people, sent forth the second proclamation concerning your negligence, or rather contempte,

492 in not laieinge open that which contrari to the good estatutes made in Parliament you had enclosed? It

In this you
showed neither
obedience nor
love of country.
If there had been
obedience you
would have put
his laws in
force; if there
had been love of
country you
[† B iv, back]
would have pre-
vented the de-
struction which
ensued.
You can see what
must follow such
oppression,
especially in a

appeareth by your doinges that there was in you neither obedience to your prince and his laws, nor loue to your contrei. For if there had ben obedience in you, you wold forthwith haue put al his laws in execution to the vttermost of youre power. And if you had loued your contrei, woulde you not haue preuented the great destruction that chaunced bi the reasone † of your vnsaciable desire? I am sure you be not rulars in your contrey, but ye can se before what is likely to folowe vpon such oppression, & especiallye in a realme that hath hertofore had a noble and a valiaunte comminalti. But graunt ye were so beastish, yet haue you not lacked them that haue tolde you of it both by wordes and writtinges. You haue ben tolde of it I saye, and haue had the threatninges of God laied plainlye before your eies, wherin you must nedes se the vengeaunce of God hanging ouer your heades for your lacke of mercy. Ther is not one storie of the Bible that serueth to declare how readi God is to take venge-aunce for the oppression of his people, but the same hath ben declared vnto you to the vttermoste ; beside the notable histories and cronicles of thys realme, wherin doeth most plainly appeare the iustice of God in the reuenging of his people, at such time as they haue kept them selues in quiete obedience to their prince & rulers, & their destruction when they haue rebelled.

Wittinglye and willinglye therfore ye haue boeth disobeied youre kinge and his lawes, and also broughte youre contrei into the miseri it is in, bi pulling vpon your self *that* vengeaunce of God whiche of his iustice he can not holde backe from such people as do *wyll-inglye and wittynglye oppresse him in his membres in such sorte as ye haue done. Howe you haue obeyed the lawes in rakeinge together of fermes, purchaisinge and prollynge for benefices, robbing the people of good ministers therby, al the world seeth, and all godly hertes lament. Loke [at] the estatutes made in the time of our late souerayne of famouse memorye Henrie the .viii. & saye if ye maye by those estatntes (taken in theyr true meaninge), either beinge no priestes nor studentes in the Vniuersities, haue benifices, or other spirituall promotions (as you call theym, for ye are ashamed to calle theym ministracions, because ye ney-ther wyll nor can minister) or beinge priestes haue pluralities of such ministrations. Well I wyl burden you no more wyth youre faultes, leaste perhappes you

CROWLEY.   10

Sidenotes:
realm which has had such a valiant commonalty.

You have been told of all this before, and must see God's venge-ance hanging over you.

There is not a story in the Bible which declares how ready God is to avenge oppression which has not been declared to you ; besides, you have the histories and chronicles of our own country, in all which God's justice is shown.

519

You have dis-obeyed the king and the laws willingly, and brought vengeance upon you.

[* B v]

526

You have pur-chased farms and benefices, and robbed the people of good ministers.

530

Look at the laws passed in the late reign, and see whether a man, being nei-ther a priest nor a student in a University, may hold a benefice, or spiritual pro-motion.

538

I will not burden you with any more faults,

but this I will say :—
You shall not sooner be gentlemen for your oppression, nor later for allowing your tenants to live by their labour; and don't think to prosper the better for your large desires.

548

[* U v, back]

You have been the cause of offence, and if it were better that he who is the occasion of one man's falling were cast into the sea, what shall be thought of you who have been the cause of so many falling ?

[¹ orig. distrube]

559

The king's blood, if he had perished, would have been required at your hands.

564

But God is merciful, and is ready to forgive all who return from their wicked ways.

569

I require you, therefore, to own your offences against the poor,
[† U vi]
who are your brothers by religion and nation.

576

can not wel beare them. But thys I shall saye vnto you :—You shall neuer the soner be gentlemen for your stout oppression, nor the later haue thynges in priuate for that ye let youre tenauntes lyue by you vpon theyre laboure. And thincke not to prospere the better in youre vnsatiable desyre, for that you tryumphe so lordelyke ouer the poore caytyfes, that, beynge seduced by the vayne hope of vyctorye promysed theym in piuyshe prophecies *haue greatly offended God by rebellion : for the greater their offence is, the greater shall your plage be when it commeth. For you haue bene the only cause of theyr offence. If he therfore that is the occasion of one mans fallyng vnto any kynd of vyce were better haue a mylstone tied aboute hys necke and be cast into the depe sea wythall, what shalbe thought of you that haue bene the occasion of so many mens fallyng into so detestable synne and trespasse agaynste God, as to disturbe¹ the whole estate of their contrei with the great perill and daunger of their anointed kyng in hys tender age, whose bloud (if he had perished) should haue bene required at your handes, as the bloud of al them that haue perished shal?

Oh merciful God, were it not that Goddes mercy is more then your synnes can be, ther were no way but to despeyre of forgeuenes ! But God is not onely mightye in mercy & able to forgeue al the sinnes of the whole world, but he is also redye to forgeue al that returne from theyr wycked wayes, and, with a constant faith & sure beleue to obtayne, do call on hym for mercye. I aduertise you, therfore, & in the name of Christ (whose name you beare) I require you, that without delaye ye returne to your hertes & acknowledge your greuous and manifold †offences, committed in your behauiour towardes the poore members of Christ (your brethren boeth by religion and nacion) whome you haue so cruellye oppressed, [and] wyshe euen from the bot-

tome of your hertes, *that* you had neuer done it. Be 577
fully determined to make restitucion of that ye haue
misse taken, though ye should leaue your selues nothynge. For better is a cleare conscience in *the* hour
of deth in a beggars bosome, then mountaynes of gould
with a conscience *that* is gilty. Wishe that you had
contented your selues w*ith* that state wherin your
fathers left you, and striue not to set your children
aboue the same, lest God take vengaunce on you
boeth sodenly when ye be most hastie to clime. And
if for youre worthines God haue called you to offyce so
that ye may wyth good conscience take vpon you *the*
state that ye be called vnto, then se you deale iustly in all
poyntes, & folowe not fylthy lucre to make your children
lordes, but studye to furnish them w*ith* al knowledge and 591
godly maners, that they may worthily succede you.

Grudge not to se *the* people growe in wealth
vnder you, neither do you inuent waies to kepe the*m*
bare, lest haply it chaunce vnto you as it did to
Kinge Nabuchedonozer[1] and hys seruauntes when
they diuised wayes to kepe the Hebrues in slauery stil. 597
*They rebelled not, but quietly did theyr labour, refer-
rynge theyr cause to God. They prepared not for
warres, neither had any confidence in theyr own
strength, but when the Egiptians thought to haue had
a faire day at them, God drowned them al in the
Redde Sea, and draue theyr deade bodies on land in
such sorte that they, whom they thoughte to kepe styll
in slauerye, myght easyly take the spoyle of them.
Thincke not therfore, but if the people quiete them
selues in theyr oppression and cal vnto God for deliuer- 607
aunce, he wyll by one meane or other geue them the
spoile of their oppressours. He is as mighty nowe as
he was in those dayes, and is now as able to slea boeth
you and youres in one night as he was to slea al the

[1] ? Pharaoh.

He fully deter-
mined to make
re-titution, for it
is better to die
poor with a clear
conscience, than
to have mount-
ains of gold and a
guilty conscience.

Content your-
selves with that
state in which
your fathers left
you, and don't
strive to place
your children
above it.
If you are called
to office, deal
justly in all
things, and do
not follow filthy
lucre.

Grudge not to
see the people
grow in wealth,

Exodi .i.

[* B vi, back]

lest God serve
you as He did
the Egyptians,
whom, when they
thought to obtain
the victory,
Exodi. xii.
He drowned
in the Red
Sea, and then
cast their bodies
on the land for
the Hebrews to
spoil.

He is as mighty
now as he was
then.

Exodi .xiiii.

612 firste borne of the Egiptyans. And then who shal haue

Be warned in
time;
the spoile? Be warned betime, least ye repente to
late! Leaue of your gredie desire to pul away the liue-

appoint good
ministers; such
as are able and
willing to in-
struct the people;
ynge from the cleargy, and seke diligentlye to set suche
ministers in the churche as be able and wyl enstruct
the people in al pointes of theyr dutie, that you with

618 them and they with you may escape the wrath of God

Ionas .iii.
that hangeth presently ouer you both. The kinge &

repent as the
Ninevites did, if
you would find
mercy, and be
[* B vii]
not ashamed to
behave as they
did.
citizens of Neniue were not ashamed to sitte in sackecloth and in ashes lamentynge their synnes, and there
vpon * founde mercye. Wherefore, if ye wyll fynde
mercye, ye muste not be ashamed to do the lyke, for
certenlye the greatnes of your sinnes importeth as

625 present distruccion to you as if ye were the same

Be not ashamed
to proclaim a
fast, and to show
to all men that
you cry for
mercy.
Come to the
temples, that men
may see you
regard Christ's in-
stitution;
give bread to the
poor, for that is
the true fast.
Niniuites that Ionas was sent vnto. Be not ashamed
ther fore to proclame a solemne fast thorowe out the
whole realme, that all at once with one voyce we may
crye vnto God for mercy. Leaue of your communions
in a corner & come to the open temples, that men may
se that ye regard the Lords institucion. Breake your
bread to the pore, that al men may se that ye regard
fastyng. For that is the true fast, to refraine the meate
& drinke that accustomably we were wont to take, &

635 geue the same (or the value therof) to the nedy. So shal
you both fele & know theyr disease, and ease it also.

Don't trust in
your warriors,
Trust not to your great number of valiant war-
riours, neither to your mightye prouisions, but re-

but remember
Holofernes
who would not
listen to the
advice of his
captain.
Iudeth .v.
member what befel to Holofernes the stout captaine
of King Nobuchodonozer, when he woulde not harken
to the right aduice of Achior hys vndercaptaine. For
certenly I say vnto you, God was neuer more redy
to deliuer his people of Israel from oppression at al

644 times when they, walkinge in his wayes, committed

God is now
ready to deliver
all Christians
who confidently
[† B vii, back]
their cause vnto him, then he is now redy to deliuer al
Christen men that do wyth lyke confidence cal vpon
him. † If you therfore wyl not hearken vnto Achior his

counsel, but determine to torment him, when ye shal
triumpth ouer the rest, doubte you not but Iudith shal
cut of al your hedes, on after another, & God shal
strike youre retinew with such a feare, *that* none shalbe
so bolde as once to tourne hys face.   Yea if there were
no men left on liue to put them in feare, they should
be feared wyth shadowes !   And though ther were no
gonnes to shote at them, yet the stones of the strete
shuld not cease to flye emonge them, by the mightye
power of God, who wyl rather make of euery grasse in
the field a man, then such as trust in hym should be
overrun or kept in oppression.   Be warned therfore, &
seke not to kepe the commones of England in slauery,
for that is *the* next way to destroie your selues !   For
if thei commit theyr cause to God & quiet them selues
in their vocacion, beyng contented with oppression, if
Goddes wyll be so ;   then shal ye be sure that God
wyll fyghte for them, and so are ye ouer matched.   But
if they wyl nedes take in hand to reuenge theyr owne
wronge, God wyll fyght agaynst you boeth, so that you
boeth, consumynge one the other, shall shortly be made
a praye to them that ye doubt least of al the world.

As you tender your owne wealth, therefore, *and
the publique wealth of thys noble realme of Englande,
which God hath enriched wyth so manye and so greate
commodities, & as you desyre to vse and enioye the
same, and not to be led away captiue into a straynge
nacion, or else be cruelly murthered among your wyues,
kinsfolke, and children, and finallye to be damned for
euer ; so loke vpon these causes of Sedicion, and do
your best endeuour to put them awaie.   You that be
oppressed, I say, refer youre cause to God.   And you
that haue oppressed, lament your so doinge and do the
office of your callinge, in defendinge the innocente and
fedinge the nedye.   Let not couetyse constraine you to
robbe the people of that porcion which they paie to

call vpon Him, but if you will not hearken, the same punishment *Iudeth .xiii. and .xv.* shall befall you as befell Holofernes, and you shall be afraid of shadows if these are no men to make you fear.

650

Be warned; seek not to keep the commons of England in slavery, lest you destroy yourselves. For if they commit their cause to God, you may be sure He will fight for them.

666

[* B viii]
As you value your own and the public wealth of this realm of England; as you desire to enjoy the same, and not be led away captive or murdered, look upon these causes of sedition, and put them away.

Let the oppressed refer their cause to God; and the oppressor lament his sin.

681

Don't rob the people of godly ministers, who

instruct them in their duty,

haue, godly ministers to enstruct them in their ductie,
and to releue the vnweldy that be not able to labour

but seek for such ministers, and let them have all the people pay.

for theire fode. Be carefull and diligent to seke for
suche ministers, and, when you haue founde them, let
them haue al that the people paye yearely out of their

689 encrease, that they may liue ther on and minister vnto
the pore out of *the* same.

So shall you escape vengeance, and be rewarded nt God's hand with plenty of all good.

Thus doinge, ye shall not onelye escape the vengeance that hangeth presentlye ouer you but also be rewarded at Goddes hande, boeth with excedinge plenti
of al good thinges in this life, & also with life euerlast-

[* B viii, back]

inge *when nature shal ende the same. Where as

If you will not take heed, you shall be more hardened than Pharaoh.

if ye wyl not take counsell, but remayne styl
in your wycked purpose, Pharao nor *the* So-
domites were neuer so hardened as you
shalbe, neyther is the remembraunce of

700 theyr distruccion so terible to vs, as
the distruccion of you shalbe to
others that shall come af-

May you by repentance

ter. The Spirite of
GOD worcke

705 in youre her-
tes, that
ye,
beynge
admonished

710 of the sword that

escape the danger.

is commynge, maye
by repentaunce
of your syn
escape

715 the daun-
ger therof.

Amen.

☞ So be it. ☜
☞

An informa-

cion and Peticion agaynst the oppressours

of the pore Commons of this Realme, compi-

led and Emprinted for this onely purpose

that amongest them that haue to doe

in the Parliamente, some godlye

mynded men, may hereat take

occacion to speake more in

the matter then the Au-

thoure was able to

write. ✳ ☜

¶ Esaye .lviii.

☞ When you suffre none oppression to bee

amongest you, and leaue of youre idle talke:

then shal you cal vpon the Lord and he

shal hear you, you shal crie, and he

shal say, Behold I am at hand.

¶ To the moste honorable Lords of the Par [leaf 1]
liament wyth the co*m*mones of the
same : theyr moste humble and
dayely Oratoure, Roberte
Crowley, wysheth the
assistence of Gods
Holy Spirite.

Monge the manyfold & moste weyghty mattiers Of all matters
(moste worthy counsaylours) to be debated to be discussed
and co*m*muned of in this present Parliament,
and by the aduise, assent, and consent therof
spedily to be redressed, I thynke ther is no 5
one thynge more nedfull to be spoken of then nothing is mot
the great oppression of the pore communes by the urgent than that
concerning
possessioners, as wel of Clergie as of *the* Laitie. No oppression of
the poor.
doubt it is nedfull, and ther ought to bee a spedy
redresse of many mattiers of religion, as are these :— 10
The vse of the sacraments and ceremonies ; the Religious matters
vsurpyng of tenthes [1] to priuate commoditie ; the super- also need to be
redressed and
fluouse, vnlerned, vndiscret, and viciouse ministers of reformed,
the church, and their superstitious and idolatrous ad- 14
ministracions. Of these thynges, I saye, ought ther to be
a spedy reformacion. For they are now most lyk hastely
to brynge vppon thys noble realme the ineuitable
vengeaunce of God, if they bee not shortly refourmed ; 18

---

[1] Orig. tuthes.

because God has made them known to us.

for asmuch as it hath pleased the almyghty and lyuyng
God to open vnto vs those abhominacions, whych
haue heretofore ben kept secret and hyd from vs.

'These thynges, I say, ar yet far out of ioynt, and
23 had great nede to be refourmed.

For notwythstandyng the Kynges maiesties late
[leaf 1, back] The ignorant people still believe
'visitacion, the ignorant people, whoe haue longe ben
fostred and brought vp in the supersticion and wronge
beleue of these thynges, and are yet, no dout, secretly‾
28 instructed by their blinde guydes and by them holden
in the super- stitions of their fathers,
styl in blyndnes, wyll not be perswaded that theyr
forfathers supersticion was not the true fayth of Christ,
tyl such tyme as they haue continuyng among them
32 such preachars as shall be able, and wyll, by the
and will ? so till better ministers are appointed.
manifeste Scriptures, proue vnto them that both they
& their fathers wer deceiued & knewe not howe to
worship God aright ; but, shamefulli seduced by the
couetyse of the shepherdes and guydes, sought hym
wher he was not ; & when they thought they had ben
38 most hygh in his fauour, by doing him such honor as
thei thought moste acceptable in hys syght, then committed they most detestable blasfemie, and were
abhominable before hym.

42   Thys knowledge, I say, wyll not be beaten into the
Ministers now are hirelings and butchers :
heads of the ignorante, so longe as theyr shepeherds
be but hyrlynges and folowe lyuynges, for such minister
not to the congregacion but to theyr owne bealyes.
They are not shepeherdes but butchars. They come
they come to be fed, not to feed :
not to feede, but to be fed. And doubtles (moste
Christen counsaylours) I thinke it not possible to
49 amende this great enormitie, otherwise then by reduce-
ynge the order of choseynge of the ministers vnto the
order that was in the primitiue church, wherof is men-
Actu. 1.
cioned in the Act. of the Apostles. For so long as ydle
bealies may come to the bishope and be smered for
Jere. 23.
money, God shall saye to them by his Prophet, " You

did renne but I sent you not." They shalle be called   [leaf 2?]
feedars of feedynge them selues, and not of fedyng 56
the flock. They shall studye to please men & not to
please God. In fine, they shall differ nothynge from they differ
the craftes men whyche applye an occupacion to get craftsmen
theyr lyuynge vppon, and not to the intent to profite
the common weale.   61

    The craftes man sueth for the fredom of a Citie, who seek for the
not because he intendeth to be a maintainer of the City,
Citie, but because he hopeth that he shall lyue so
muche the more welthyly hym selfe. And euen for 65
lyk causes do our ministers, and are lyke styll to do because they will
(so longe as they maye bee receyued when they come be better off.
vncaled), applye them selues to priestyng, because they
lyke wel the ydelnes of the lyfe.

    I doubt not but the Kynges maiesties visitters
knowe more of thys matter then I can be able to 71
wrytte. And by them, I doubte not, you shall bee
moued to commone of thys mattier at the full.

    The sacramentes they styll abuse, vseing them as The Sacraments
matters of merchaundyce, and chiefly the most worthy are still abused;
memorie of our redemption; for that they selle boethe 76
to the quycke and to the deade, to the rych and to the
poore. None shall receyue it at theyr handes wythout they must be
he wyll paye the ordinarie shotte, and so are they redy paid for, and
to serue euery man. Thei loke vppon the monei onely then every man
and nothynge vppon the mynde. Whether it be taken may have them.
to comfort of conscience or iudgement, they pas not; 82 upon the money
thei tel the monei, thei loke for nomore. If they wyll They know this
deny this to bee true, let them saye why they suffer is true,
the pore to begge money to paye for theyr housel, as
they call it? Perchaunce they wyll answer that the but excuse them-
money is not payede for the sacrament, but for the iiii selves by saying
offeryng dayes? Then aske I this questian :— the money is not
    Why thei appoint not another time to receiue it in Sacraments, but
then that tyme whyche is to lyttle to bee occupied in for the four

collect the money at some other time. declareynge to the people the right vse & profyte of the sacramentes, & to instructe them, so *that* they do

93 not receyue it to theyr iudgment, but to theyr confort and quietnes of conscience, for whych purpose it was

But they take it then because they will make sure of it. first instituted ? Vndoubtedli (most Christia*n* counsailours) they can not deny but that they appoynt to receyue it then because they wyll be sure of it.

98   Theyr doeynges wyll declare it thoughe they

The Sacrament is administered irreverently, and only to such as pay. woulde deny it, for none may receyue the sacramentcs vnles he do fyrste paye the money. And then, wyth how lyttle reuerence it is ministred and receyued, euery Christen hert sceth & lamenteth.

103   These thynges (I doubt not) are so euident and playne vnto you that it nedeth not to troble you wyth

Many men write and preach against these abuses; so that there is just reason to seek for further redress in the Parliament. manye wordes concerneynge· the abuses therof. Many godly mynded men haue boeth writton and preached, & do dayely write and preach, of and agaynst those abuses ; wherfore I am certen that you haue iuste occacion and can do no lesse but scke a furder redres herof (whych all Chrysten hertes do desyr) in thys present

111 parliament.

I fear the oppression of the poor will be passed over in silence, But as for the oppression of the pore, whych is no lesse nedfull to be commun*e*d of and reformed then the other, I feare me wyll bee passed ouer with silence, or if it bee communed of, I canne scarsely truste that

116 any·reformaciou canne bee had ; vnlesse God do nowe worke in the hertes of the possessioners of thys realme,

[leaf 3] unless God move the hearts of the possessioners to sell their lands. as he dyd in the primitiue church, when the possessioners wer contented and very wyllynge to sell theyr possessions and geue the price therof to be commune to al the faythful belcuers. Take me not here that I

I do not advocate a community of goods. shoulde go about by these wordes to perswade men to make all thynges commun*e* ; for if you do, you mistake

I mean no such thing. me. For I take God to wytnes I meane no suche thynge. But with all myne herte I woulde wysh that

126 no ma*n* wer suffered to eate but such as woulde labourc

in theyr vocacion and callyng, accordynge to the rule
that Paule gaue to the Thessalonians.

2 *Thess.* 3.

But yet I woulde wysh that the possessioners
woulde consyder whoe gaue them theyr possessions,
and howe they ought to bestowe them. And then (I
doubt not) it shoude not nede to haue all thynges
made commune.

But I would
have the posses-
sioners remem-
ber who gave
them their
possessions
and what for.

133

For what nedeth it the seruauntes of the housholde
to desyrre to haue theyr maysters goods commune, so
longe as the stuarde ministreth vnto euery man the
thynge that is nedefull for hym?

137

If the possessioners woulde consyder them selues to
be but stuardes, and not Lordes ouer theyr possessions,
thys oppression woulde sone be redressed. But so
longe as thys perswasion styketh in theyr myndes,—
"It is myne owne ; whoe shall warne me to do wyth
myne owne as me selfe lysteth?"—it shall not bee
possible to haue any redresse at all. For if I may do
wyth myne owne as me lysteth, then maye I suffer my
brother, hys wyfe, and hys chyldrene to lye in the
strete, excepte he wyll geue me more rent for myne
house then euer he shal be able to paye. Then may I
take his goods for that he oweth me, and kepe his body
in prison, tournynge out his wyfe and chyldren to
perishe, if God wyll not moue some mans herte to pittie
them, and yet kepe my coffers full of goulde and syluer.

Possessioners are
only stewards,
not lords, and
there can be no
redress

143

while they think
they may do as
they will with
their own.

148

[leaf 3, back]

152

If ther were no God, then would I think it leafull
for men to vse their possessions as thei lyste. Or if
God woulde not require an accompt of vs for the
bestoweynge of them/, I woulde not greately gaynsaye,
thoughe they toke theyr pleasure of them whylse they
liued here. But forasmuch as we haue a God, and he
hath declared vnto vs by *the* Scripturs *that* he hath
made the possessioners but stuardes of his ryches, and
that he wyl holde a streygh[t] accompt wyth them for
the occupiynge and bestoweynge of them ; I thynke

If there were no
God then it might
be lawful to use
possessions thus;

157

but there is a
God, and He has
made possessors
stewards only.

162

1 3

163 no Christian ears can abyde to heare that more then Turkysh opinion.

The Philosophers said friends should possess in common:

The Philosophers who knewe nothyng of the bonde of frendshippe which Christe our Maister and Redemer lefte amonge vs, affirmed that amonge frendes al thynges are common, meaneyng that frendshippe woulde

169 not suffer one frende to holde frome an other the thynge that he hath nede of. And what shal we saye? Are we not frendes? Surly if we be not frendes, wee beare the name of Christe and bee called Christians in

if we haven't more perfecte friendship than they we are not true Christians.

vayne. Yea if wee haue not a more perfecte frende-shyppe then that whereof the Philosophers speake, wee are but fayned Christians, we beare the name onely

176 and are nothynge lesse in dede. For this is the token that Christe gaue whereby wee shoulde be knowen

John .13.

to be of hym:—"If we loue one an other as he loued vs." Howe he loued vs is declared by the wordes of

Ephes. 5.

the Apostle, sayinge, that Christe gaue hymselfe for vs.

[leaf 4] If we follow Christ's example we shall not spare ourselves, but shall give our lives for the good of others.

Accordynge to this exemple ought our frendshyp to be such, that we wyll not spare to spende our lyfe for the welth of our brothers. Not to fyght in theyr quarell (for Christe bade Peter put vp the swerde into his place), but to teach the truth boldly, without any feare

186 of death, and not to suffer oure brothers to bee led in erroure, thoughe presente death shoulde insue for so doynge.

Some, perchaunce, wyll thynke that this frendshyp is to be vnderstande onely of the pastors and shep-

John .10.

herdes towarde theyr flocke; because Christ sayth that

192 a good shepherde geueth his lyfe for his shepe. For-

This friendship refers to the laity and clergy,

sooth if the pastours or shepeherdes onely were the flocke of Christe, then myght thys frendeshyp ryght well be vnderstanded of them onely. But for asmuch

because both belong to the flock of Christ.

as the laie and priuate persons ar as well of the flocke of Christe as the other, thys frendeshyp parteineth vnto them no lesse then to the other. And thys causeth

me (moste worthy counsaylours) not to feare the dis- 199
pleasure of men in this behalfe; knoweynge for cer- *This makes me fear man's displeasure.*
tentie, that the greateste numbre of thys assemble are
not free from this oppression that I speak of, and that
it is far vnlyke that a priuate persone, by no meanes
worthy to be called to suche an assemble, shoulde be 204
fauourably hereade and accepted of them whom God
hath called to be counsaylours of a realme; and
chiefly in a cause taxynge & blameyng the iudges
befor whom it is pleaded. I might well coniecte wyth *For speaking in this manner I may be counted a busybody, but I am ready to suffer*
my selfe, that I shoulde in this poynte be compted a
busy body,[1] and one that renneth before he is sent.
But I am redi to suffer, not onli al such report, but
euen the verye death also (if it shall please the al- *[leaf 4, back]*
mightie and euerlyueynge God to laye it vpon me) for *anything for your sakes.*
youre sakes, most worthy counsaylours, and the residue,
my naturall brothe[r]s of this noble realme. 215

And here I proteste vnto you all, that the same *The Spirit that sent Christ and the prophets*
Spirite that sent Ionas to the Niniuits, Daniel to the
Babilonians, Nathan to Kyng Dauid, Achior vnto
Holofernes, Iudith vnto the Priestes and Elders of the
Iewes, the prophete to Ieroboam in Bethel, Iohn the 220
Baptist vnto Herode, and Christ vnto the Iewes, wyt- *witnesses that I am sent*
nesseth wyth my conscience that I renne not vnsent.
For euen the same Spirit that sayd vnto Esaie, "Crye *Esaie. 58.*
and sease not, declare vnto my people theyr wyckednes;" cryeth also in my conscience, bydyng me not 225
spare to tell the possessioners of this realme, that vn- *to tell you possessors to repent of your oppressions, and show yourselves brothers, of one father, and members of one body.*
lesse they repente the oppression wherewyth they vexe
the pore commons, and shew themselues, through loue,
to be brothers of one father & membres of one body
wyth them, they shal not at the laste daye enherite
wyth them the kyngdom of Christe, *the* Eldest Sonne 231
of God the Father, whych hath by his Worde be-
gotten hym many brothers & coheritours in[2] his kyng-
dom. Vnlesse, I saye, the possessioners of this realme *Unless you all repent of the*

---

[1] Orig. boby   [2] Orig. is

violence done to the poor, you will be cast into outer darkness.

wyll repent the violence don to the poore and nedy membres of the same, and become as handes, ministryng

238 vnto euery membre hys necessaries, they shall, at the daye of theyr accompt, be bound hand and fote and cast into vtter da[r]cknes, wher shal be wepyng, wealyng, and gnashyng of teeth; that is, dolour and payne, the greatnes wherof canne not be expressed

[leaf 5] wyth tonge nor thought wyth herte. And thys much

Esaie. 59.

Unless you make the poor to cease from crying, God will not prosper your reformations, but will leave you in the power of the prince of this world.

more sayeth the Spirite. Vnlesse ye purge your selues of this bloude, & stop the mouthes of the pore that the voyce of theyr complayn[t]e come not vnto myne eares, I wyl not prospere your counsayles in the reformacions of those abhominacions which I shewed vnto you, but wyll leaue you to the spirite of errour, the prince of thys worlde, whose dearlinges ye are so longe as ye seke not the welth of the nedy, but your

251 owne priuate commoditie.

These thynges hath the Spirite of God spoken. Heauen and earth shal perish, but the wordes of the

Now hear what complaints are made against you in heaven:

Spirite shall not perysh, but be fulfylled. Nowe herken you possessioners, and you rich men lyfte vp your ears; ye stuards of the Lord, marke what complayntes are layede agaynste you in the hygh court of

258 the lyueynge God.

Lord, hast thou forgotten us ?

"Lorde" (sayeth the Prophete) "hast thou forsaken vs? Doest thou hyde thy selfe in the tym of our trou-

While the wicked man grows proud [See Psalm x.] the poor are afflicted.

ble? Whylse the wycked waxe proud the pore man is aflicted and troubled. Would to God the wicked

Would God the wicked might feel some of the troubles he invents for others.

myght feale the same thinges that they inuent for other. For the sinner prayseth hym selfe in the desyres of hys soule, and he extolleth and sette[t]h forth the couetouse man. He prouoketh the Lorde and

267 is so proud that he wyll not seke hym. He neuer thynketh vpon God. His wayes be defyled at all tymes. He loketh not vpon thy iudgmentes, Lorde, he

270 wyll reuenge hym vpon all hys enimies.

"He thynketh thus wyth hym selfe, I wyll not re- | He thinks he shall remain.
moue frome one generacion vnto an other wythout
mischiefe. His mouth is full of malediction and euill | He is full of fraud and deceit.
reporte, fraude & deceyte, and vnder his tonge is affliction
and iniquitie. | 275

"He lyeth in wayte wyth the riche men of the | [leaf 5, back.] He lies in wait in villages to
villages or graynges, in secrete corners, to the intent to | slay the innocent, to take the poor
slea *the* innocent. Hys eyes are fyexed vpon the pore ; | man ; and when he has taken
he layeth awayete euen as a lyon in his denne. He | him he uses him violently.
layeth awayte to take the pore man by force, and when
he hath gotten him within hys reache, then wyll he
take hym violentlye. In hys net will he ouerthrowe | 282
the pore, and through hys strength shall the multitude
of the oppressed be ouer charged and fall. For in his | He says God has forgotten and has
herte he sayeth, God hath forgotten, God turneth a | turned away His face.
waye hys face, and wyll neuer regarde the oppression of
the pore," etc., to the ende of the same Psalme. | 287

What sentence (thinke you) wyll the Lorde geue
vpon this euidence? No doubt (most worthey coun-
sellers) euen the same that we reade in Esaye the | *Esaie.* 5.
Prophet : — "I loked for iudgment and rightouse
dealeynge amongeste my people, and beholde there is | 292
iniquitie, I loked also for iustice, and beholde ther is
an outcrye. Wo be vnto you therfore, that do ioyne | The sentence God will give
house vnto house, & couple one fielde to an other, so | against those who join house to
longe as there is any grounde to be had. Thinke you | house and field to field ; against
that you shal dwel vpon the earth alone? The Lorde | such as oppress instead of dealing
of hostes (sayth the prophete) hath spoken these wordes | justly :—
vnto me. Manye large and goodlye houses shall be | Many houses shall be desolate,
deserte & without inhabitantes ; x acres of wynes | ten acres of vines shall only yield
shall yelde but one quarte of wine, and xxx bushelles | one quart, and 30
of sede shal yelde but x bushelles agayne." Beholde, | bushels of seed shall only yield
you engrossers of fermes and teynements, beholde, I | ten.
saye, the terible threatnynges of God, whose wrath you | 304
can not escape. The voyce of the pore (whom you

CROWLEY. 11

13 ★

[leaf 6]

haue with money thruste out of house and whome) is

307 well accepted in the eares of the Lorde, and hath

You cannot escape God's threatenings.

steared vp hys wrath agaynste you. He threateneth you most horrible plages. Ten acres of vynes shal yelde but one quarte of wyne, and xxx bushelles of

The seed of God's Word shall remain barren in your hearts.

sede but x bushelles agayne. The sede of Goddes Worde sowen in youre hertes shalbe barrayne and not bringe fourth fruite.

314   For couetous, the rote of all yuelles, occupieth that grounde so that the heauenlie sede can bi no meanes geue encrease. This is a plage, of al plages most

God will punish you "lease mongers" who take lands that you may let them out again,

horryble. And doubt ye not, you lease mongers, that take groundes by lease to the entente to lette them out agayne for double and tryple the rent, your parte is in this plage.[1] The Lorde shal take his Spirite from you.

321 He shall forbyd the cloudes of hys mercy to rayne vpon

and you surveyors, that of ten-pound land make twenty.

you wyth the swete dwe of hys grace. And you sur-ueighers[2] of landes, that of x. li. lande can make xx, you shall not be forgotten in the effucion of thys plage.

When you have raised your rents to the highest,

For when you haue multiplied your renttes to the higheste, so that ye haue made all your tenantes your

327 slaues to labour, and toyle, and bringe to you all that maye be plowen and digged out of youre groundes,

you'll die suddenly, and God's grace will be taken from you,

then shal death sodaynly strike you, then shall God wythdrawe his comfortable grace from you, then shall your conscience prycke you, then shall you thynke

332 with desparat Cain, that your sinne is greater then that

and you will think yourselves unworthy of mercy, because you have shown no mercy.

it may be forgeuen. For your owne conscience shall iudge you worthye no mercye, because you haue shewed no mercy. Yea the same enimie that hath kendled and doeth yet maynetayne in you thys mischeuouse,

[leaf 6, back]

outragiouse, and vnsaciable couetousnes, shall then bee as busy to put you in mynde of the wordes of Christ, saienge, "*the* same measure that you haue made vnto

340 other, shalbe nowe made vnto you."

[1] Orig. palge   [2] Orig. surneighers

You haue shewed no mercye, howe can you than 341
loke for mercie ? Oh noble counsailours, be mercyfull
to your selues. Destroye not your owne soules to en- Do not destroy
riche your heires. Enlarge not your earthly posses- your souls to
enrich your
sion wyth the losse of the eternall enheritaunce. heirs.
Learne to knowe the estate that God hath called you 346
vnto, & to lyue accordinge to your profession. Know
that you are al ministres in the common weale, and Remember you
are ministers in
that the porcion which you are borne vnto, or that the commonwealth.
your prince geuethe you, is your estate. Knowe that Your duty is to
distribute, and
your office is to distribute & not to scrape together on not scrape
heapes. God hath not sette you to surueye hys landes, together.
but to playe the stuardes in his householde of this 353
world, and to se that your pore felow seruantes lacke
not theye[r] necessaries.

Consider that you are but ministers and seruauntes You are only
servants, and
vnder the Lorde oure God, and that you shal render a will have to give
streyght accompt of your administracion. Stand not an account of
your adminis-
to much in your own conceyte, gloriynge in the worthy- trations.
nesse of your bloude ; for we are all one mans chyl- 360
dren, and haue (by nature) lyke ryght to the richesse
and treasures of thys worlde, whereof oure natural
father Adame was made Lord and Kinge. Which of
you can laye for hym selfe any naturall cause whye he
shoulde possesse the treasure of this wor[l]de, but *that* 365
the same cause may be founde in hym also whome you
make your slaue ? By nature (therefore) you can By nature you
can only claim
claime no thynge but that whiche you shall gette with [leaf 7]
the swet of your faces. That you are lordes and what you earn.
gouernoures therfore, commeth not by nature but by the That you are
lords comes by
ordinaunce & appoyntment of God. Knowe then that ordinance, not by
nature.
he hath not cauled you to the welthe and glorie of this 372
worlde, but hath charged you wyth the greate and rede
multitude.

And if any of them perishe thorowe your defaute, If any poor
knowe then for certentye, that the bloude of them perish through
Ezech. 33.

your neglect, their blood will be required at your hands.

shalbe required at your handes. If the impotent creatures perish for lacke of necessaries, you are the murderers, for you haue theyr enheritaunce and do 380 minister vnto them.

If they steal, you are the cause, because you have enclosed all the lands.

If the sturdy fall to stealeyng, robbyng, & reueynge, then are you the causers therof, for you dygge in, enclose, and wytholde from them the earth out of the whych they should dygge and plowe theyr lyueynge.

Psal. 113.

For as the Psalmiste wryteth :—" All the heauen is the Lordes; but as for the earth hee hath geuen to the 387 chyldrene of men."

The whole earth therfor (by byrth ryght) be-longeth to the chyldren of men. They are all in-heritours therof indifferently by nature.

You are ap-pointed to give meat to God's household.

But because the sturdy shoulde not oppresse the weake and impotent, God hath apoynted you stuards to geue meate vnto his housholde in due seasone. And if 394 you be founde faythfull in this littel, then knowe that he wyll preferre you to much greater thinges. But if ye bee founde oppressing your felowe seruauntes, then knowe for certentie, that the Lorde your Maister shall at hys comeynge rewarde you wyth many strypes.

Luke .12. Daniel .4. [leaf 7, back] Remember Nebuchadnezzar, who became a beast,

Call to your remembraunce the History of Kynge Nabuchodonosor, whoe for his presumption became as a brute beast, fead[ing] vpon grasse and hey as other beastes dyd.

403 Consyder Pharao with his great armie, whom the Lord ouerwhelmed in the Red Sea for oppresseyng and

and Pharaoh, whom the Lord drowned in the Red Sea.

persecuteyng his people. Yea, consider all the nobilitie that haue possessed the erth, euen from the begynyng ; and then saye howe you bee theyr successours, & by what title you may cleyme that which was theyrs.

The Romans held all Europe and part of Africa and Asia, and where are their successors ?

Many hundred yeres sence the noble Romains helde all Europa and parte of Affrike and Asia in quiete pos-session ; and where are they that succeade them in theyr impier ?

The brutishe Gothes inuaded and vanquished the Who are the successors of the Goths? impier of Rome ; and wher are theyr successours?

What shoulde I stande in the rehersale of the **415** greate possessioners that haue hertofore possessed the erth, whose lynial descent can not be founde? It shall suffice me to remyt you to the wordes of the Lorde vnto Nabuchodonosor, whyche are written in the boke of Daniel the Prophete. *Dani. 4.*

Ther shall you learne that it is God that geueth All empire is from God, and He gives it to whom He will, as Christ said to Pilate. the impiere to whome it pleaseth hym, and that all powre is from aboue, accordynge to the answer that our sauioure Christe made vnto Pilate, when he bragged **424** hym wyth the powre that he had to crucifie hym and to deliuer hym.   " Thou shouldest," sayed our Sauiour, *John .19.* " haue no powre ouer me at all, were it not geuen the from aboue." **428**

Thus is it euident vnto you (moste worthy coun- Thus it is clear all your power and property come from above. [leaf b] saylours) that your powre and estate cometh frome aboue ; and that by nature you can cleyme nothynge of the possessions of this worlde, more then that whyche you gette wyth the swet of your faces. **433**

I doubt not therfore but that your consciences do I do not doubt but that in your consciences you agree to what I have said. condesende and agre vnto that which I haue spoken concernynge your office and ministerie; knoweynge that God hath appointed you to minister necessaries to the impotent, and to defende the innocent. **438**

Do not therfore neglect thys principalle poynt of Do not neglect your duty, but redress this oppression. your dutie, to seke in this parliament a redresse of thys great oppression, wherwyth the pore membres of this noble realme ar most vnmercifully vexed on euery side.

The lande lordes for theyr partes, suruey and make Landlords make the uttermost penny of their grounds, besides fines and incomes; *the* vttermost peny of al their growndes, bysydes the vnreasonable fynes and incomes, and he that wyll not or can not geue all that they demaunde, shall not enter, be he neuer so honest, or stande he neuer so greate neede.

Yea, though he haue ben an honeste, true, faythfull **448**

and quiete tenant many yeres, yet at the vacation of his copie or indentur he must paye welmoste as muche as woulde purchayse so much grownde, or else voide in hast, though he, his wyfe and chyldrene, shoulde

453 perishe for lacke of harbour.

What a sea of mischifes hath floued out of thys more then Turkyshe tyranie! What honeste housholders haue ben made folowers of other not so honest mens tables! What honeste matrones haue ben brought to the needy rocke and cardes! What men-

459 chyldrene of good hope in the liberall sciences, and other honeste qualities (wherof this realme hath great

lacke), haue ben compelled to fal, some to handycrafts, and some to daye labour, to sustayne theyr parents decrepet age and miserable pouertie! What

464 frowarde and stoubourn children haue herby shaken of the yoke of godly chastisement, rennyng hedlonge

into all kyndes of wickednes, and finaly garnyshed galowe trees! What modeste, chaste, and womanly virgins haue, for lacke of dourie, ben compelled, either

469 to passe ouer *the* days of theyr youth in vngrate scruitude, or else to marye to perpetuall miserable pouertie!

What immodeste and wanton gyrles haue hereby ben made sisters of the Banck (the stumbling stock of all frayle youth) and finaly, moste miserable creatures,

lyeinge and dieynge in the stretes ful of all plages and penurie! What vniuersall destruction chaunceth to this noble realme by this outragious and vnsaciable desyr of the surueiers of landes! I reporte me to you (moste Christian counsayellours) which ar here assembled from all partes of this noble realme, to consulte for the

480 welth of all the membres of the same.

On the other syde, ther bee certayne tenauntes, not able to be laude lordes, and yet, after a sorte, they conterfayte landelordes, by obtaynyge [1] leases in and

---

[1] Orig. obtaynydge

vpon groundes and tenementes, and so reyse fynes, 484
incomes, and rentes ; and by suche pyllage pyke out a
porcion to mayntayne a proude porte, and all by
py·lynge and pollynge of the poore commons, that must
of necessitie seke habitations at their handes. 488

That this is true, I report me to my Lorde the
Maire, and other the hed officers of the Citie of London, whoe (if they be not ignorant of the state of the
Citie) can witnes with me that the moste parte, yea I
thinke ix of the x partes, of the houses in London
bee set and let by them that haue them by lease and
not by the owners. 495

Nine-tenths of the houses in London are let in this way. [leaf 9]

Howe thei polle the pore tenantes would sone be
tryed, if theyr leases were conferred with theyr rent-
rolles. It is not to be thought contrary but that the
greate leasmungers haue greate gains by their leases, for
the litleons, that hold but a piece of houseing of xx. or
xxx s. by yere, can fynde the meanes to holde and dwell 501
vpon the chiefe parte therof rent fre, by letynge out
the residue for the whole yerely rent.

How they impose upon the tenants would soon be seen if the leases and rent-rolls were compared.

I thinke not contrary, but these thinges do appeare
in the syght of many to bee but verey trifles, and not
worthy to be spoken of in so noble an assemble as this
most honorable Parliament. For they are no mattiers
concerneyng the welth of the nobilitie ; yea it is rather
hyndrance to many of them, to haue these thynges
redressed, then any encrease of theyr wealth. 510

These things appear to be trifles which do not concern the nobility and seem to be unworthy of notice by the Parliament.

Yea euen you (moste Christian counsaylours) whych
are here assembled to debate tho weightie mattiers of
thys realme, are not all so free from this kynde of
oppression, but that you coulde be well contented to
wyncke at it. And therfor, for asmuche as the inor- 515
dinate loue of men towarde them selues is such, that
eyther they can not se theyr owne fauts, or else if they
do se them or be tolde of them, they take them not to
be so great as they are in dede ; I thinke it no 519

Even you, Christian Councillors, are not all so free from this oppression, but you would rather wink at it ;

so I shall not
wonder if you
laugh at my fool-
hardiness and
[leaf 9, back]
rashness in
entering upon
this subject,
because men do
not agree to such
things as will
diminish their
profits.
meruayle, though such of you (most worthy counsaylours) as haue any profite by this oppression, do wythin
them selues deride and laugh to scorne my fole hardi-
nes and rashe enterpryse herein, knoweynge that it is
not the vse of them that bee assembled to the intent
to establish such thynges as shall be for the welth of a
whole realme, to condescende and agree to those
thynges whych shallbe disprofitable vnto the chiefe
528 membres of the same.

Truth it is (moste worthy counsailours), I myght
well and worthyly be laughed at if I woulde attempte

What I have
said is for the
profit of the
whole realm.
any suche thynge. But the thynge that hytherto I
haue spoken of is not to the disprofite of any, but to
the greate commoditie and profite of all the whole
534 realme.

For what discommoditie is it to the heade, shoul-

The upper mem-
bers of the body
should clothe the
lower members
from any harm
which might
happen to them
in their carrying
the body about,—
ders, the armes, and other the vpper membres of the
body, beynge all redy sufficiently clothed, to put on the
legges & feete a peare of hose and shoes to defende
them also from the iniuries of the wether, and other
hurtes that might chaunce vnto them in theyr trauayl-
541 ynge to cary the body from place to place, for hys
commoditie and pleasure? Verily in myne opinion,
that body is far vnworthy to haue either legges or
feete that wyll lette them goe bare, haueynge wher-
545 wyth to couer them.

so you, the chief
members, should
provide for those
members beneath
you, and give
them a portion of
the riches which
you possess.
Euen so you, beynge the chiefe membres of this
noble realme, and haueing in your handes the wonderful and incomparable riches of the same, what shoulde
it greue you to departe wyth some porcion therof, that
the inferioure membres therof may at all tymes bee
551 able to do theyre ministerie and office accordyngly.

Bear in mind
that the body
without the legs
is only like a
[leaf 10]
block, and cannot
move; so you, if
Once remembre, that as the body wythout the in-
feriour partes is but lame and as a blocke vnweldy, and
muste, if it wyll remoue frome place to place, creepe
vpon the handes; euen so you, if ye had not the pore

membres of this realme to tyll the grounde and doe your other droudgery, no remedy, you must nedes do it your selues.

you had not the poor to till the ground, must do it yourselves.

Vse them therfore as the necessarie membres of the mistical body of this most noble realme, and be not in this poynt mor vnnatural then the heathen Philosophers were.

Therefore you must use the poor as members of this realm, else you will be more unnatural than the heathen,

They in theyr writtynges declare no lesse then I haue here written.

564

This ought not a lytle to moue you, beyng Christians (whose Redemer, Iesu Christ, sitte[t]h at the right hande of God his Father) to study, not onely to be equale wyth, but to pas the heathen and vnchristined in this mattier, euen as farre as the excellencie of the name and religion which we professe passeth theyrs.

whom, as Christians, you ought to surpass.

570

Remembre (most Christian counsaylours) that you are not onely naturally membres of one bodi with the pore creaturs of this realme, but also by religion you ar membres of the same misticall body of Christe, whoe is the heade of vs all (his membres), and estemeth all that is done to the leste of vs his membres as done to hym selfe. For he sayeth :—

By religion you are all members of Christ's body,

574

and Christ esteems what is done to His members as done to Himself.

"What so euer ye do to one of the lest of these litleons that beleue in me, ye doe it vnto me." If you therfore, neither wil your selfes oppresse our Sauiour Christe in his membres, nor suffer other to do it, fayle not to fynde a redres of this greate oppression, whych I haue declared to the same ende. And then I doubt not but God shall so worke wyth you, that euerie man shall wyllyngely embrace a reformacion of all mattiers of religion. For the Spirit of God shall dwell in you and in vs all, and Christe himself (as he hath promised) shall bee in the myddes amonge you. Wher as, contrariwise, if you suffer our loucinge Sauiour thus to be oppressed, he wyll forsake you, he wyll leaue you to the spirite of errour. Your reformacions shal take no

Mat. 25.

If you will not oppress Christ through His members, redress these wrongs, and then every man will assist you in reforming religion.

584

[leaf 10, back]

If you oppress the poor, Christ will forsake you and leave you to a spirit of error.

592 place. All your diuises shall be abhominable in his syght, because ye haue not purged your handes from the bloude of this oppression.

Let the decres whych were establyshed in thys place by a Parliament assembled for a lyke purpose be your president, not to folow, but to beware by them that ye establish not the lyke.

The intent of that assemble was no lesse to refourm the abuses of our religion then thys is. But because Christe was not deliuered frome oppression he woulde

602 not be amonge them.

They were not congregated in hys name, but rather agaynste hym and hys doctrine, for he hym selfe is dear loue, & (as his Apostle Iohn writeth) wher this dear loue is not, ther is not he. Thys thynge is well

607 proued by theyr proceadynges in the same Parliament.

For they established Articles euen directly agaynst Gods worde, forbedynge to mary, and commaund- ynge to put asunder those that God hath ioyned to- gether.

If you wyll call these Articles into question agayne (as in dede you haue iuste occacion to do) I doubt not but you shal be fully perswaded that they proceaded of

615 the spirit of erroure, and not of the Spirite of God ; because the charitie of God was not amonge them in that assemble.

Other thynges therbe wherby the pore membres of Christe in thys noble realme are oppressed ; wherof I haue made no mention, partely because I am loth to offende wyth the multitude of my rude wordes, & partely for that I know you can not seke for a redres of these thynges wherof I haue spoken. But the other wil offer them selues vnto you, I meane the greate ex- tortion and vsurie that reigneth frely in thys realme, and some to be authorised by Parliament wythin these

627 .iii. yeres laste paste.

The Cleargie of the Citie of London haue, for theyr parte, optayned by Parliament authoritie to ouertenthes euen after the exem[ple] of the landlordes and leasemongers, and maye, by the vertue of the acte, requir for double rentes double tenthes. If the rent of any kynde of housyng or grounde wythin the Citie of London be raised (as ther is in dede veri much) from x.s to xx.s, than may the persone (whoe had before but xvi.d.ob.), by the vertu of this act demaunde .ii.s. ix.d, the double. Bysydes this, the exactions that they take of the pore commons is to much beyonde al reason and conscience. No couple can be maried but these men must haue a dutie, as they cal it. No woman may be purified but they and theyr ydle ministers must haue some duties of hir. None can be buried but they wyl haue a slyese. Not thre monethes before the begynyng of this present Parliament, I had iust occacion to be at the payment of this dutie for the buriyng of an honest pore man, whose frendes wer willyng to haue hys body reuerendly layed in the grounde; and, accordyng to the custome, gaue warnynge to the curate that they woulde brynge the deade body to the church, desyryng hym that he wolde do hys dutie, and to be ther to receye it, and accordynge to the custome to laye it in the grounde. But this rauen, smellynge[1] the carion, coulde not but reueile it to the other carion byrdes of the same chur[c]h, and so woulde needes come all together in a flocke to fetch theyr praye, wyth crosse and holy water as they were wont to do, not wythstandynge the Kynges Iniunctions and late visita[t]ion. The freudes of the deade man refused all this, and required to haue no mor but the commune coffen to put the bodye in, agreynge to paye to the keper therof hys accustomed dutie, and in lyke maner to the graue maker, and the

the clergy over-tithe, and for double rent demand double tenths.

631

636

They exact money from the poor

for marriages,

churchings,

642

burials.

(How the clergy acted at St Sepulchre's Church

648

[leaf 11, back]

652

in the City of London,

657

when an honest poor man

was brought to be buried

' Orig. smellydge.

foure pore men to cary the bodye, so that the whole
664 charges had ben but vii.d.

in St Sepulchre's,
London.)
But when the corps was buried, wythout other
crosse or holy water sticke, Dirige, or Masse, wyth
prayers of as small deuocion as any pore curate could
saye, yet must we nedes paye .vii.d. more.   That is to
669 saye .i.d. to the curate, which he called an heade
penye,[1] and .vi.d. to .ii. clarkes that we had no nede of.

This was done in
London, and I am
ready to prove
the truth of the
statement any-
where.
This was done in Sepulchres paryshe in the Citie
of London.   And if it shall please any of thys noble
assemble to trye the trueth of this, I wyll verifie it
where so euer I shall be called, euen in the presence of
675 all the ydle ministers of the same church.

I have mentioned
this circumstance
because I think
we ought to have
ministers sup-
ported by tithes,
or else be allowed
[leaf 12]
to do the duties
ourselves.
This haue 1 written (most worthy counsaylours) to
geue you occasion to set suche an ordre in this and
suche other thynges, that eyther we may haue ministers
founde vppon the tenthes that we paie yerli to the
churches, other els that it may be leafull for vs to do
such ministeries our selues, and not to be thus con-
682 strained to feede a sorte of carion crowes, whyche are
neuer so mery as when we lament the losse of our
frendes.

Thus much of the
extortion of the
clergy.
This much haue I spoken of the extortion that
reigneth frely in the Clergie.   Nowe, with your
I will now speak
of the usury
which prevails.
pacience, I wil, with like breuitie, speak of the great
and intollerable usurie, whych at this daie reigneth so
689 frely this realme ouer al, and chiefly in the Citie of
London, that it is taken for most leaful gaines.   Yea
It is almost
heresy to speak
against it because
it is allowed by
Parliament.
it is welmost heresie to reproue it, for men saye it is
alowed by Parliament.   Well, the most parte, I am
sure, of this most Godly assemble and Parliament do
The Act was
passed on ac-
count of the
greed of the
usurers, and
interest was
limited to ten
per cent.
knowe that the occasion of the acte that passed here
concernynge usurie, was the unsaciable desyre of the
usurers, whoe coulde not be contented with usurie
vnlesse it wer vnreasonable muche.   To restrayne thys

[1] Orig. pedye

gredy desyre of theyrs, therfore, it was communed and 698
agreed vpon, and by thauthoritie of Parliament de-
creed, that none should take aboue .x. li. bi yere,[1] for
the lone of an .C. li.

Alas, *that* euer any Christian assemble shoulde bee
so voyde of Gods Holy Spirit *that* thei should alowe
for leafull any thyng that Gods Worde forbedeth.
Be not abashed (most worthy counsaylours) to call this 705
act into question agayne. Scan the wordes of the
Psalmist concernyng this mattier. " Lord," sayeth he,
" who shal enter into thy tabernacle, and who shal rest
in thy holy mountaine ? " He answereth : " That
entreth w*ith*out spot & worketh righte. That speaketh
truth in his herte, & hath not deceiued w*ith* his tonge ;
that hath done his neybour no harme, nor accepted any
reproch against his neibour. He regardeth not the 713
wicked, but them that feare the Lorde he glorifieth and
prayseth. He that swereth to his neibour & deceiueth
hym not. He that hath not geuen his money vnto
vsury, and hath not take*n* giftes and rewardes against
the innocent." 718

If you (most Christian counsaylours) do glory in
the knowledge of Gods Spirite, whoe hath spoke*n*
these wordes by the Prophet, how can you suffer this
acte to staude, whych shalbe a wittnesse agaynste you
in the later daye that you alowe that which Gods
Spirite forbideth ?

If he that geueth not hys money to usury shal 725
dwell in the Lords tabernacle, wher shal he dwel that
geueth his money to usuri ? Shal he not be shut out,
& caste into vtter darcknes ? Their workes be contrary, & why shoulde not theyr rewarde be also contrary ? If the one be receyued in, the other muste be
shut out. Yea, and you that haue made this lawe,

----

[1] See *Supplication of the poore Commons*, ed. J. M. Cowper, p. 84, ' Men myghte take x li. by yeare,' &c.

Marginal notes:

Alas, that any Assembly should allow what God forbids!

Consider the subject again, *Psal.* 14. and see what the Psalmist says. From his words, the man who does not give his money upon usury shall enter heaven. [leaf 12, back]

How can you allow this Act to stand ? It shall be a witness against you in the Last Day.

Usurers must be shut out of heaven, and those who made the law allowing

14

usury, unless you revoke it.
vnlesse you do reuoke it and establysh an act to the contrary, the Brydegroume, the onely Sonne of God,

731

Math. 7.
shal at the laste daye deny you, and saye that he neuer knewe you; "Depart from me," shal he saye, "al ye workers of iniquitie." Scanne the wordes of the Prophete therfore, and scanne the wordes of oure

738 Sauioure Christe also, in the vi. of Luke, wher he

Christ bids you lend, looking for nothing again, and you shall be the children of God.
sayeth thus :—"Do you lende[1] lokynge for no gaynes therof, and your rewarde shalbe plentuouse, and you shall be sonnes of the Hygheste, because he is gentle & liberal toward the vnthankfull and wicked."

743

Men have wrested this [leaf 13] saying, and made it no precept, but only a counsel of Christ.
I am not ignoraunt what glosses haue ben made vpon this place, and howe men haue wrested & made it no precept but a counsaile of our Sauiour; & therfore not to infer necessitie to Christians, but to leaue them at libertie either to do it or leaue it vndone.

What religion do these men profess ?
Oh mercifull Lorde, what maner of religion is it that these men professe?

They boast them selues to bee the disciples of

751 Christe and setters forthe of his glorie.

They bear Christ's name, and yet think they may choose whether they will follow His counsel or not; those who do not hear His voice are none of His;
They wyll beare the name of hym and be called Christians, and yet wylbe at libertie to chose whether they luste to folowe hys counsayle or leaue it vndone.

Our shepherd Christe, of whose flocke they boaste them selues to bee, sayeth that hys sheepe heare his voyce and folowe hym.

John .10.
And immediatly before he sheweth the cause why the Iewes dyd not credyt hys wordes, to be none other

760 but that thei wer not his shepe.

but they who teach that men are at liberty to practise Christ's counsels or not, as they may see fit, are
And doubte ye not (moste worthy counsaylours) what so euer he is that wyll defende or teach, that any one lytle iote of the counsayles of Christ shoulde be so vaynly spoken that any of hys flocke myght refuse to

765 practise the same in hys lyuynge to the vttermoste of

members of the devil and very Antichrists.
hys power, is nolesse then a membre of the Deuell, and a verey Antichriste.

¹ Orig. lenve.

For he that desyreth not in hys herte to practise in 768
his lyueynge all the counsayles of Christe our Maister
and Teachar, shall be numbred amonge the obstinate *and shall be numbered with*
Iewes for none of the flocke of Christ, because he *the Jews.*
heareth not his voice nor foloweth him. Thus I mak
an ende. 773

Wyshyng vnto you (most worthy counsaylours) the *May the Spirit*
same Spirit that in the primitiue church gaue vnto the *which dwelt in the primitiue*
multitude of beleuers one herte, one mynde, & to *Church dwell in [leaf 13, back]*
esteme nothyng of this worlde as theyr owne, minis- *Actu. 4.*
you, and cause
trynge vnto euerie one accordyng to his necessities; *you to make a*
law preventing
that you, led by the same Spirite, may at the lestweye *oppression; and*
ordeine such a lawe that the oppresion of the pore 780
reigne not frely amonge them that beare the name of
Christians. But if they wyll be styll oppressyng the *if men will still*
oppress let such
pore membres of Christ, after once or twyse admoni- *be called Mam-*
monists and not
cion, let them no more be named Christians after Christ *Christians.*
whom thei serue not, but Mammonistes after Mammon
whose badge they beare. And this reformacion had, no 786
doubt the maiestie of God shall so appere in all your
decrees, that none so wicked a creatur shalbe founde so
bolde as once to open his mouth against the ordre that
you shal take in al matters of religion. Yea, the verie
enimies of Dauid shall do omage vnto Solomon for 791
his wisedom. Al the Kynges christined shal learne at *Then all kings*
shall learn of you,
you to reforme theyr churches. You shalbe euen the *and you shall be*
the light of the
light of al the world. *world.*

But, if you let these thynges pas and regarde them *If you do not,*
not, be ye sure the Lorde shal confound your wisdome. *God will confound*
your wisdom, no
Inuent, decre, establysh, and authorise what you can; *matter what you*
decree.
al shal come to nought. The wayes that you shall 798
inuent to establish vnitie and concorde shal be the
occacions of discorde. The thynges wherby you shal
thinke to wyn prayse through all the worlde, shall
turne to your vtter[1] shame; and the wayes that you shall 802

---

[1] Orig. vnter.

803

God gire you His Spirit.

inuent to establish a kyngdome shalbe the vtter subuertion of the same. The mercifull Father of our Lorde Iesus Christe indue you wyth hys Spirit, that you be not partakers of these plages.

Amen.

Amen.

GLOSSARIAL INDEX.

Abye, 51/1524, abide, expiate.
  Disparage not the faith thou dost
    not know,
  Lest, to thy peril, thou *aby* it dear.
    Mid.-Sr. N. Dr. iii. 2, l. 176
    (Globe ed.).

Agime ziphres, 73/571 ?

Allayes, 9/137, 10/161, alleys.
  Bowling-alleys in which the game
  of bowls was played; alleys, lanes
  or courts in the city of London.

Allyes, 132/84, alleys.

Apointe, 137/273, arrange with.

Armore, 18/426, ? armourer.

Ascoye, 43/1271, askew, askance,
  side-ways.

Babbelars, 103/119.   See Acts
  xvii. 18.

Bable, 32/884, bauble.

Baliwike, 43/1257, the jurisdic-
  tion of a bailiff.

Ballyng, 83/27, bawling.

Banck, 166/472, sisters of the
  Bank, prostitutes, inhabitants of
  Bankside.

Barre, to cast the bar, 73/33.
  See *note*, p. xvii.

Base, to run base, 73/35.   See
  note, p. xvii.

Bealies, 132/92, bellies.

Bearwardes, 17/388.

Beastish, 144/505, beastlike,
  brutish.

Bested, 60/19, circumstanced.
  See *Chaucer, C. T.*, 5069, and
  Isaiah viii. 21.

Betrusted, 30/823, trusted.

Bisemeyng, 95/14, beseeming.

Bityme, 72/66, betimes, in time.

Bler, 70/12, blear.

Brast, 132/8, burst.

Breuitie, 172/687, brevity.

Bridle-rayne, 95/6, bridle-rein.

Brynke, 16/364, brink, brim.

By, 101/75, be.

By yere, 173/700, for a year.

Byll, 29/800, bill, a petition.

Candle, to hold the, 130/21, phr.

Cardes, 166/458 ?

Cessions, 94/143, sessions.

Checkinge, 139/348.

Christined, 175/792, christened.

Cocke and Pye, 19/469, a petty
  oath. See *Merry Wives of W.* i. 1,
  l. 316 (Globe ed.).

Coheritours, 159/233, coheirs.

Commone, 155/73, commune.

14 ★

Commotionars, 22/555, commotioners, men who cause commotious or tumults.

Condynge, 81/63, condign, "that is, according to merit, worthy, suitable." *Phillips.*

Coniecte, 159/208, conjecture.

Cormerauntes, 131/69, cormorants.

Costnouse, 91/30, costly.

Couetise, 26/690, covetousness.

Crake, 81/62, crack, boast of.

Crowmes, 132/95, crumbs.

Days, offering days, 155/88, certain days on which offerings were made to the Church.

Dearlinges, 160/249, darlings.

Destituted, 132/104, made destitute, deprived.

Dirige, 172/666.

Disconforte, 111/81, discomfort.

Disprofitable, 168/527, unprofitable.

Dorepostis, 111/93, door-posts : "deaf as a door-post," a common phrase.

Dyprease, 32/898, dispraise.

Earely, 94/134, early.

Eer, 88/91, ever.

Effucion, 162/324, effusion.

Emong, 12/239, among.

Entermel, 32/904, intermeddle.

Euerychone, 89/113, each one, every one.

Fere, 88/76, in fere, in common.

Forestall, 34/972, to buy goods on their way to market.

Forestallers, 34/965, men who bought corn or cattle or goods of any kind as they were on their way to a market or fair, and then sold them again at a higher price.

Forlore, 99/131, lost.

Fryses, 33/933, friezes, woollen cloths or stuffs originally from Friesland.

Gate, 44/1275, gait.

Gossepes, 103/142, gossips.

Graue maker, 171/662.

Graynges, 161/277, granges.

Gulles, 131/69.

Hadland, 13/266, headland.

Harbour, 113/140, shelter.

Haulke, 73/29, hawk.

Head penny, 172/669.

Herbour, 8/99, harbour, shelter, lodging.

Herte rote, 19/464, heart root.

Houseing, 167/500. *See* Housynge.

Housel, 155/85, the Sacrament.

Housynge, 116/271, shelter, houses—probably for *housen*, an old plural of house still in use in Northamptonshire.

Imperye, 99/137, empire, rule, power.

Ioynt, 154/22, joint. Phr., "out of joint."

Iuell, 19/454, evil.

Leafull, 157/153, lawful.

Lestweye, 175/779, "leastways."

Lette, 139/328, let, a hindrance.

Leyes, 50/1500, leys, leas, pastures for cattle.

Lite, 88/70, little.

Litleons, 167/500, 169/579, little ones.

Liuear, 140/378, liver.

Liuelode, 65/51, livelihood.

Loselles, 112/121, lozel, a lazy lubber.

Luste, 174/754. See Lyste.

Lynge, 13/276, ling, saltfish. Consult *The Babees Book* for information about ling and fish generally.

Lyste, 157 154, list, like, choose.

Malt, 114/201.

Mammonists, 175/785.

Markis, 116/251, a Mark was of the value of 13s. 4d.

Maugrea, 62/86, maugre, in spite of.

Mawe, 44/1294, maw, stomach.

Meaners, 101/75, manners, ? demeanours.

Mell, 20/494, meddle.

Morysh, 119/370, marshy.

Mowe, 9/132, mow, a stack of corn.

Mownde, 112/110, a boundary.

Noble, 80/52, a coin of the value of 6s. 8d. See *Four Supplications*, Glossary in v. *noble*.

Nownde, 112/110, for mound, a fence or hedge — boundary.

Omage, 175/791, homage.

Other, 172/665, either.

Ouertenthes, 171/630, to over-tithe, or over-tax.

Packe, 11/193, number.

Paisant, 141/423, Paisaunte, 142/460, peasant.

Pardye, 123/502, *Par Dieu*, a common oath.

Pas, 155/82, heed, care.

Paste, 45/1316. The 'paste wife' was probably the woman who made the *pasts*, *partlets*, or ruffs then much worn. "Gay gownys and gay kyrtels, and mych waste in apparell, rynges, and owchis, wyth partelettes and *pastis* garneshed

wyth perle." More's *Suppiycacyon of Soulys*, sig. L. ii., quoted in Halliwell's *Arch. Dict.*

Peltrye, 46/1366. The word *pelt* is still in use in Kent, signifying *rubbish*, the sense in which *peltrye* is used here.

Plowen, 162/328, plowed.

Pold, 13 277, polled, robbed, cheated, polling, 20/506.

Poppyshnes, 72/71, popishness.

Porte, 167/486, bearing, carriage, or manner.

Possessioners, 153/8, holders of large estates.

Praye, 148/669, prey.

President, 170/597, precedent.

Priestyng, 155/68, the calling or duties of a priest.

Primer, 71/55, a little book, which children are first taught to read. *Phillips.*

Prollynge, 144/529, prowling, searching about.
  Prolyng, and pochyng to get somwhat
  At euery doore lumpes of bread, or meat.
    R. Copland's *Hye way to the Spyttel Hous.*

Prouender, 141/379. "Provender pricketh them," a phrase used in *Newes out of Powles*, Sat. 6:
  1st meruaile though they cranckly crowe
  well lodged in their cage?
  With *prouen prickt, yst* meruaile now
  That thus the Tigars rage?
The modern equivalent, applied to a restive horse, is "the oats prick him."

Pryme, 91/23, prime, 6 a.m., one of the seven canonical hours.

Pyld, 13/278, pilled, spoiled.

Quyte, 69/222, requite. See 1 *Tamb. the Great*, ii. 5.

Reade, 32/894, 84/58, counsel, advice.

Rede, 163/373, ? scattered. Halliwell has *Rede* (3), to spread abroad.

Regester, 78/12, ? registrar.

Reueynge, 164/381, ravening, taking by force, from the verb *to reve*.

Rocke, 166/458, a distaff.

Route, 91/6, to rule the rout, to rule the common people.

Royall, 20/502, royal, or rial, a coin of the value of 10 shillings, first coined in the reign of Hen. VI. In the reign of Hen. VIII. the gold rial was ordered to go at 11s. 3d. In the 2nd of Elizabeth rials were coined at 15s. In the 3rd of James I. rose-rials of the value of 30s. were coined, and spur-rials at 15s. each. The *rial farthings* went at 2s. 6d. each in the reign of the "Tiger King."

Salfe, 102/93, safe, or saved.

Scan, 173/706, 174/736.

Scase, 81/72, scarce. See Glossary to *England under H. VIII.*

Schourges, 15/344, scourges.

Shamefast, 131/53, shamefaced, modest.

Shente, 38/1096, 86/24, ruined, destroyed.

Shote, 155/79, shot, amount.

Slyese, 171/643, slice.

Smered, 154/53.

Spittlehouse, 11/211, hospital.

Stick, holy water stick, 172/666.

Stockefyshe, 13/276, stockfish, saltfish dried. For much curious information concerning *Stockfish*, see Mr Furnivall's *Babees Book*.

Stynt, 112/108, stint, stop.

Swea, 94/133, sway, bear the sway, have rule.

Tatyllars, 103/117, tattlers. See 1 Tim. v. 13.

Thral, 87/32, make men thral, enthrall men.

Thyne, 80/32, thin, weak.

Tipillyng, 71/33, tippling.

Tussocke, 44/1303, a heap.

Typpet, a Tyburn tippet, 30/820, a halter.

> To weare . . . .
> A *Tiburne Tippet*, or old Stories cap.
> This is the high'st degree which they can take.
>> Taylor's *Works*, fol. 287.

Vaile, 17/392, avail, profit, advantage.

Vitayls, 8/90, victuals.

Vnchristined, 169/568, unchristened, unbaptized.

Vndercaptaine, 147/641.

Vngrate, 166/469, ? unbecoming.

Vnweldy, 168/553, unwieldy.

Wede, 113/140, clothing.

Wel, 61/68, weal.

Welmoste, 10/166, almost, well nigh, nearly.

Whippets, 45/1331, ? short petticoats. See Halliwell's *Arch. Dict.*

Wit, 55/8, blame.

Wodmonger, 88/75, a dealer in wood.

Yuelles, 162/314, evils.

Ziphres, Agime ziphres, 73/571?

GENERAL INDEX.

Richard Clay & Sons, Limited, London and Bungay.